THE CANMORES

KINGS & QUEENS OF THE SCOTS 1040-1290

THE CANMORES

KINGS & QUEENS OF THE SCOTS 1040-1290

RICHARD ORAM

TEMPUS

First published 2002

PUBLISHED IN THE UNITED KINGDOM BY:

Tempus Publishing Ltd
The Mill, Brimscombe Port
Stroud, Gloucestershire GL5 2QG
www.tempus-publishing.com

PUBLISHED IN THE UNITED STATES OF AMERICA BY:

Tempus Publishing Inc.
2 Cumberland Street
Charleston, SC 29401
(Tel: 1-888-313-2665)

www.tempuspublishing.com

British Library Cataloguing in Publication Data.
A catalogue record for this book is available from the British Library.

ISBN 0 7524 2325 8

Typesetting and origination by Tempus Publishing.
PRINTED AND BOUND IN GREAT BRITAIN.

Contents

Thanks to Michael Penman for contributing the section on Margaret the 'Maid of Norway'.

THE CANMORE DYNASTY

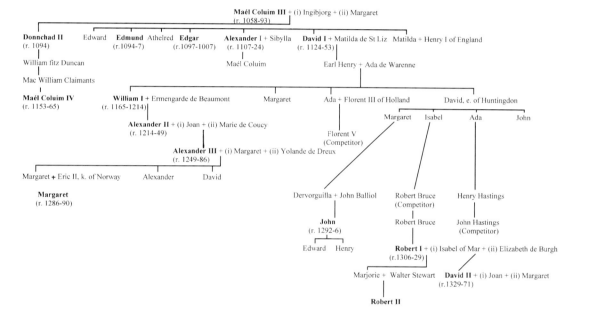

Maél Coluim III + (i) Ingibjorg + (ii) Margaret
(r. 1058-93)

Donnchad II   Edward   **Edmund** Athelred **Edgar**   **Alexander** I + Sibylla   **David I** + Matilda de St Liz Matilda + Henry I of England
(r. 1094)   (r.1094-7)   (r.1097-1007)   (r. 1107-24)   (r. 1124-53)

William fitz Duncan   Maél Coluim   Earl Henry + Ada de Warenne

Mac William Claimants

Maél Coluim IV   **William I** + Ermengarde de Beaumont   Margaret   Ada + Florent III of Holland   David, e. of Huntingdon
(r. 1153-65)   (r. 1165-1214)

                                                                  Margaret Isabel   Ada   John

Alexander II + (i) Joan + (ii) Marie de Coucy
(r. 1214-49)   Florent V
                                                  (Competitor)

Alexander III + (i) Margaret + (ii) Yolande de Dreux
(r. 1249-86)

Margaret + Eric II, k. of Norway   Alexander   David   Robert Bruce   Henry Hastings
                                       Dervorguilla + John Balliol   (Competitor)

Margaret
(r. 1286-90)   Robert Bruce   John Hastings
                                                    John   (Competitor)
                                             (r. 1292-6)

                                                 Edward   Henry   **Robert I** + (i) Isabel of Mar + (ii) Elizabeth de Burgh
                                                                   (r.1306-29)

                                               Marjorie + Walter Stewart   **David II** + (i) Joan + (ii) Margaret
                                                                  (r.1329-71)

                                                          Robert II

2. Edward the Confessor as depicted in a wooden screen, *c*.1500, of St Catherine's Church, Ludham, Norfolk. Malcolm III had strong ties with England, journeying to Edward's court possibly to renew the oath of former Scottish rulers to be 'sworn helper' of the English kings.

Introduction:

A Prince in Exile

In the year 1040, Donnchad mac Crinain (Duncan I), king of Scots, led an army into Moray against his kinsman and rival, Macbethad (Macbeth). Far from being the elderly and respected king of Shake-spearean tradition, Donnchad was a young and not particularly talented man, whose reign had stumbled from crisis to disaster since he had succeeded his grandfather as king in 1034. At Pitgaveny near Elgin, Donnchad was defeated and killed and Macbethad ascended the throne as king of Scots. Despite his triumph in battle, however, Macbethad's position was never to be entirely free from challenge, for Donnchad's sons had been spirited away to safety in exile. The future might bring a reversal of fortune.

While Máel Coluim, the elder of Donnchad's sons, lived in exile in England, Macbethad's opponents looked to the dead king's adult relatives for alternative leadership. In 1045, Donnchad's father, Crinan, raised a rebellion that probably aimed to place his younger son, Maldred, on the throne. But Macbethad crushed the rising and killed Crinan. The following year, the English king Edward the Confessor, under whose protection young Máel Coluim was living, sanctioned an invasion of Scotland by Earl Siward of York. Máel Coluim, who was living in Siward's household, however, is unlikely to have been the candidate that Edward planned to set on the Scottish throne, for he was probably barely into his teenage years. More likely it was his uncle, Maldred, who was set up as ruler following Siward's defeat of Macbethad. The latter, however, was a formidable opponent and before the year's end he had returned to destroy the man who had displaced him. It was to be the last challenge to Macbethad's rule for several years.

By 1054, Máel Coluim, now in his twenties, was regarded by Edward the Confessor as head of the Scottish royal kindred and the best candidate for advancement as a dependable vassal on the Scottish throne. Siward was once again permitted to launch an invasion of Scotland in support and, after a bloody battle, succeeded in wresting control of the country south of the Forth from Macbethad. But Macbethad was still in control of the heartland of his kingdom and Máel Coluim faced a long struggle to assert his power. In 1057 at Lumphanan in Aberdeenshire, he again confronted Macbethad in battle. This time, although Macbethad's army may have been victorious, the old king died of his wounds. Máel Coluim, however, was unable to prevent his enemies from securing the inauguration as king of Macbethad's step-son, Lulach, and he was forced to mount a second offensive the following year. At Essie in Strathbogie, Lulach and his army were overwhelmed and Máel Coluim the exile returned in triumph to assume the throne of his forefathers.

1

MALCOLM III OR
MÁEL COLUIM MAC DONNCHADA

(1058-1093)

Máel Coluim mac Donnchada, who as king of Scots is better known by the anglicized form of his name, Malcolm III, would not have known in 1058 how permanent his victory over his dynastic rivals was to prove. A ruthless and opportunistic warrior, he stamped his authority over Scotland and was to maintain an unshakeable hold on power for thirty-five years. It was possibly this unquestioned might that won him his nickname, Ceann Mór (Canmore), 'Great Head' or 'Great Chief', from which the dynasty he founded, which ruled Scotland for nearly two and a half centuries, receives its name. With ambitions to match his ruthlessness, Malcolm III used his security at home to project his power abroad, deservedly earning himself a reputation as one of Scotland's greatest warrior kings.

Despite the years that he had spent in exile in England, Malcolm won quick acceptance from the powerful Gaelic nobles of his still predominantly Gaelic kingdom. His Gaelic character appears to have been unblunted by long exposure to Anglo-Saxon culture and there was no trace of the anglicizing influence that was to become such a feature of his later years. If anything, the foreign influences that he had absorbed in his years abroad were Scandinavian in character, the product of his long sojourn in the York court of his Anglo-Danish patron, Earl Siward. English ties, however, remained strong and in 1059, perhaps mindful of the debt owed for past support, Malcolm journeyed to the court of

3. York. For some fifteen years, Malcolm was a refugee at the court of
Siward, Earl of York and Northumbria.

Edward the Confessor, possibly to renew the oaths of former Scottish
rulers to be 'sworn helper' of the English kings. By 1061, however,
Malcolm was prepared to kick over the traces and, despite being the
'sworn brother' of the current Northumbrian earl, Tostig Godwinsson,
took advantage of Tostig's absence on pilgrimage at Rome to launch a
devastating raid through his territories. Peace was restored and Tostig
was later to find refuge at Malcolm's court when driven out of his
earldom in 1065, but this first raid signalled the direction that the Scot's
true ambitions were to follow throughout his long reign.

Lasting security on Malcolm's northern frontier was won by c.1065
through his marriage to Ingibjorg, widow of Thorfinn the Mighty.
While her sons ruled in Orkney there was peace between the Scots and
the Norse. Nothing is known of their relationship other than that the
marriage produced two children, Donnchad (Duncan) and Domnall
(Donald), before Ingibjorg's death in about 1069. Her death opened
fresh prospects for the widowed Malcolm, for by 1070 fate had brought
to his shores a shipload of Anglo-Saxon exiles fleeing the most recent
failed rising against the Norman conquerors of England. In the ship
were Edgar Atheling, the Anglo-Saxon claimant to the English throne,
his mother and his sisters Margaret and Christina. It was a heaven-sent

4. William the Conqueror invaded Scotland in 1072 (although there were no pitched battles) to force Malcolm III to expel Anglo-Saxon exiles from Scotland. Fifteenth-century depiction in stained glass.

opportunity for Malcolm, for marriage to one of the sisters offered the prospect of a realization of his ambitions to extend his influence southwards, an ambition baulked that same year when his attempt to capitalize on the weakened state of Northumbria following William the Conqueror's systematic devastation of the north was bloodily repulsed. Furthermore, there was the chance that a son of such a union would some day succeed to the English throne should the West Saxon dynasty be restored. For Edgar, it was a price worth paying for safe refuge and a powerful military ally. Even though both his sisters had – if Margaret's biographer, the Benedictine monk Turgot who served as her chaplain and confessor, is to be believed – intended to become nuns, he persuaded the elder, Margaret, to accept.

An understanding of the implications of this marriage may have been the catalyst that persuaded William the Conqueror that he had to bring Malcolm to heel. In 1072, William invaded Scotland by land and sea but there was no battle. Instead, at Abernethy on the Tay, Malcolm submitted to the Norman king, promising to expel the Anglo-Saxon exiles, performing homage and surrendering his eldest son, Donnchad,

5. Newcastle, Tyne and Wear. William the Conqueror's son, Robert Curthose, built the first castle here as a safeguard to curb Malcolm's ambitions.

as hostage. For seven years he kept his word, then in 1079, drawn by the apparent collapse of Norman royal power in northern England, he launched a devastating raid into Northumbria. In 1080, William sent his eldest son, Robert Curthose, to subdue Malcolm but the campaign ended in a conference at Falkirk that ostensibly renewed the terms of the 1072 treaty. Often presented as a defeat for Malcolm, this settlement marked the high watermark of his power, for, as Robert's hasty building of a castle at what became Newcastle-upon-Tyne revealed, Malcolm had successfully pushed his frontier far to the south. Indeed, he had come close to rebuilding the old Northumbrian realm of Bernicia that stretched from the Forth to the Tees. The dream of consolidating the Scottish hold over this southern realm was to be a chimera pursued by Malcolm and Margaret's descendants until the thirteenth century.

Marriage to Margaret marked a decisive shift in the cultural influences on Malcolm. Instead of the Scandinavian element evident down to 1070, Anglo-Saxon culture now predominated. This is clearest in the names given to the first four of Malcolm and Margaret's sons – Edward, Edmund, Æthelred and Edgar – named after the queen's male progeni-

6. Queen Margaret's Chapel, Edinburgh Castle, Edinburgh. The late eleventh- or early twelfth-century chapel has long been associated with the queen, who died in the castle in 1093, but was probably built in the reign of her son, David I.

7. Dunfermline Abbey, Fife. The first Benedictine Abbey in Scotland, founded by Malcolm III and his saintly wife, Margaret.

8. The coat of arms of Henry I and Matilda of Scotland. Matilda (or Edith as she was called before her marriage to Henry I in November 1100) was the daughter of Malcolm III, King of Scots.

tors from father to great-great-grandfather respectively. There was more to the move than fashion, however, for the children were probably being groomed to take their place in England after the expected revolt that would drive the Norman usurpers into the sea.

Opinion varies as to the extent of Margaret's influence over Malcolm and his policies. The number of Anglo-Saxon exiles in Scotland was small, but concentrated at court their influence was disproportionately great. As queen, Margaret was in a stronger position than any to influence her husband, but Malcolm was not an altogether unwilling subject. The king was not blind to the opportunities offered by his marriage and he may have been keen to ensure that his sons were schooled in his wife's foreign ways to smooth their future acceptance to the English. Indeed, Malcolm evidently considered that the future lay with his sons by Margaret, for he passed over his sons by Ingibjorg to designate Margaret's eldest child, Edward, as his chosen successor. Turgot suggests that the king venerated her every act and supported her efforts to introduce the culture and sophistication of the Old English monarchy to his rough and ready court. Certainly, she brought a veneer of continental urbanity to the Gaelic household, introducing Anglo-Saxon and Frankish clothing and hairstyles, court ceremonial and refined tableware. More contentious, however, are suggestions that she initiated profound change in Scottish religious life. What is clear is that Margaret, brought up in the spiritual hothouse of recently-converted Hungary and having experienced at first hand the tide of religious reform that was transforming the Western Church, found the native church in Scotland disturbingly backward in its practices and distressingly poorly organized to offer the level of pastoral care that she considered normal. With Malcolm's support – he is reported to have acted as her interpreter – she assembled the leading Scottish clerics in a bid to instigate reform, and it seems that some limited success was achieved. To aid in the reform process, again with Malcolm's support, she wrote to Archbishop Lanfranc of Canterbury to request that he send a colony of Benedictine monks to form the basis of a monastery to be founded beside the royal stronghold at Dunfermline. It was a faltering start, for the priory at Dunfermline had barely put down roots when its monks were expelled in the political upheavals that followed the king's death in 1093. Rather than Margaret, it was her sons who were to carry through her dreams of religious revival.

Despite Margaret's efforts to polish her husband, Malcolm remained an inveterate warlord in the Gaelic tradition. Ever the opportunist, in 1091 he took advantage of William II's absence in Normandy to launch

9. Tynemouth Priory, Tyne and Wear. Following his death at Alnwick, Malcolm's body was first brought here for burial before its eventual return to Scotland.

a plundering raid into England. Retreating in the face of the inevitable retaliation, led by William and his brother Robert in person, Malcolm once again made an easy submission, offering his homage and fealty in return for William's promise to restore properties formerly held by the Scottish kings in England. The apparent generosity of the terms despite Malcolm's repeated breaches of faith should not mask the fact that Norman power in the north had grown considerably since the 1070s, and when in 1092 William took control of Carlisle, where he built a castle and started a programme of colonization, that power reached the borders of Malcolm's kingdom. Perhaps confident of his new-gained authority in the north, William baited Malcolm by repeated failure to implement his side of the 1091 agreement. In August 1093, Malcolm travelled to Gloucester in a final bid to secure William's fulfilment of the treaty. Possibly in a deliberate move to provoke Malcolm into again breaking his word, William slighted him. Infuriated, Malcolm returned to Scotland, swiftly raised an army and in early November, accompanied by his son Edward, invaded Northumbria. Bogged down by the rain and mud, Malcolm was outmanoeuvred by the Norman earl and on 13 November was ambushed and killed near Alnwick. The Scots fled, taking with them the seriously wounded Edward, who died of his injuries two days later near Jedburgh, but leaving the king's body behind on the field. On 16 November, gravely ill, her body worn out by the demands of at least eight pregnancies and by the rigours of a life of fasting and self-denial, Margaret received the news she had dreaded shortly before she herself died.

2

DONALD III OR
DOMNALL MAC DONNCHADA (1094-1097)
DUNCAN II OR
DONNCHAD MAC MÁEL COLUIM (1094)
AND EDMUND (1094-1097)

The death of Malcolm III, his designated heir and Queen Margaret in the space of four days in November 1093 unleashed a backlash against the Anglo-Saxon influence that had dominated the Scottish court since the 1070s. The chief beneficiary was Malcolm's younger brother, Domnall mac Donnchada (Donald III), nicknamed *Bàn* – the White or Fair-Haired – known from Shakespearean tradition as Donaldbane. Beyond the tradition that when Malcolm had fled to England in 1040 he had instead gone west to the Norse-Gaelic kingdom of the Isles, nothing is known of his life until his sudden emergence in old age as the figurehead in this violent reaction against foreign influence. As the eldest surviving adult male of the family, Gaelic tradition would have marked him out as Malcolm III's heir, but it had clearly been his brother's intention to exclude him in favour of the sons of his second marriage. This break with tradition may have been the catalyst that united the opposition to Malcolm's family behind Domnall mac Donnchada, but there is next to no record of how his coup was mounted. Later hostile chronicle accounts speak of his invasion of the kingdom, siege and capture of Edinburgh Castle, and expulsion of his brother's surviving children. With his nephews all in exile, Domnall was enthroned as king at Scone, probably early in 1094.

The first challenger to Domnall's position was his eldest nephew, Donnchad, better known under his anglicized name, Duncan, the

10. Gaelic Sunset. Tradition reports that Domnall Bàn had found refuge with the Norse-Gaelic rulers of the Hebrides after the killing of his father in 1040.

11. King Duncan II depicted as a mounted Norman knight on his great seal.

12. Iona Abbey, Argyll and Bute. Donald III was the last Scottish king reputed to be buried on the holy island.

surviving son of Malcolm III by his first wife, Ingibjorg. Duncan, who in 1072 had been handed over as a hostage to the English king, William the Conqueror, had largely been brought up at the Norman court in England, schooled in English ways and trained as a Norman knight. On the Conqueror's death in 1087, Duncan had been released and knighted by the new king, William II Rufus, but had opted to remain in England. For William, Duncan offered an unparalleled opportunity to establish a pliant vassal on the Scottish throne, thereby ending the twin threat of Scottish support for rebels in England and Scottish challenges on his northern frontier. Having given oaths of homage and fealty to William, and bolstered by marriage to Octreda, daughter of the former Northumbrian earl, Cospatric, whose family were powerful figures in the shifting borderlands between the kingdoms, Duncan marched north with an army of Normans and English. In May 1094 he defeated Domnall and his supporters in battle and was enthroned as King Duncan II. His grasp on power, however, was short-lived. Within a few months, a coup had forced him to dismiss his foreign soldiers while permitting him to retain the throne, but on 12 November 1094 he was murdered at Mondynes near Stonehaven by Maelpedair, ruler of Mearns. Octreda fled to England with their son, William, and before the year's end Domnall had been re-established on the throne.

The defeat and death of Duncan opened the fault lines in the family of Malcolm III. Early in 1095, Edmund, the eldest of Malcolm's surviving sons, opened negotiations with his uncle and secured a share of power. Domnall had at least one daughter – Bethoc – but no sons, and Edmund, as his eldest nephew, may have been recognized as his successor. Edmund's actions evidently alienated the rest of his family, and when Domnall and Edmund gave their support to the rebel Norman earl of Northumberland, William Rufus passed over Æthelred – still alive but for some reason seen as unsuitable – and threw his weight behind Edmund's younger brother Edgar as a rival for the Scottish throne. After a long struggle, in 1097 Domnall and Edmund were defeated in battle and captured. Edmund was at first consigned to chains and imprisoned, but subsequently became a Cluniac monk and died in obscurity in Montacute Abbey in Somerset, safely removed from his former kingdom. History records a more gruesome fate for Domnall, who was blinded at the urging of his youngest nephew, David. His date of death is unknown, but tradition narrates how he was permitted to live until 1107, when he was killed on the instructions of King Alexander I. First buried at Dunkeld, his remains were later translated to Iona, a more fitting resting-place for this last king in the Gaelic tradition.

3

EDGAR

(1097-1107)

In 1095, passing over his elder brother Æthelred, William Rufus, king of England, selected Edgar, fourth son of Malcolm III and Margaret, as his candidate for the Scottish throne. Edgar, who had been living in exile at the English court since late 1093, had accompanied William north on his 1095 campaign against Robert de Mowbray, the rebel earl of Northumberland, and had been invested by him with the kingship of the Scots at this time. Edgar, however, was in no position yet to turn his title into a reality. Around him was gathered a group of exiled Scots opposed to Domnall mac Donnchada, but his key ally was his uncle Edgar Atheling, the Anglo-Saxon claimant to the English throne. It was only in 1097 with the Atheling's aid, at the head of a largely English army, that Edgar returned to Scotland to wrest the throne from his uncle and brother.

After the violent upheavals of the previous years, Edgar's reign appears to have been a time of comparative peace. A potential threat to this stability had been removed in 1098 when he settled a treaty with Magnus Barelegs, king of Norway, which recognized Norwegian sovereignty over the Hebrides, averting conflict with a king who was intruding his authority into western maritime Britain. His apparent willingness to yield sovereignty of an area that had once formed the political and spiritual core of his ancestral kingdom, however, underscores the fact that Edgar, despite his Gaelic blood, was very much a

13. Coldingham Priory, Borders. Edgar gave the lands of Coldingham to the monks of Durham.

14. Durham Cathedral, Tyne and Wear. Edgar was a noted patron of St Cuthbert's community.

15. Seal of Edgar.

product of the new English orientation of his family. Indeed, he has been likened to an Anglo-Saxon rather than a Scottish king. There is no evidence that he visited the north or west of his kingdom and he had little sympathy for or understanding of Gaelic culture and society. Edgar instead reinforced a southward-focused perspective by new ties with England, in particular by the marriage of his sister Edith (also known as Matilda) to the English king, Henry I. This attitude can also be seen in his religious policies. In 1098, he granted Coldingham to the monks of Durham – he attributed his victory the previous year to St Cuthbert's intervention – and was present when the foundations of a new church were laid there. He also brought monks from Canterbury to recolonize Dunfermline, which he began to rebuild.

In 1107, still only in his early thirties, Edgar died. There is no record of his ever having married and the throne passed to his younger brother Alexander. His body was taken to Dunfermline, where it was buried alongside his parents in front of the high altar of the church.

4

ALEXANDER I

(1107-1124)

Like his brothers before him, Alexander I succeeded to the throne as a vassal of the English crown. His dependence was emphasized by his marriage to Sibylla, one of Henry I's brood of bastards, a woman described in Scottish chronicles as lacking in both modesty and looks. Henry made great use of his illegitimate children as instruments for strengthening his power, frequently arranging for the marriage of his daughters to nobles whom he wished to bind more firmly in their loyalty to him, or to magnates who occupied key positions on his frontiers. Alexander fitted into just this category and the marriage, a simple act of policy, evidently remained loveless and childless.

New tensions within the family had surfaced soon after Alexander's accession. While the throne passed by right to Alexander, Edgar had apparently bequeathed much of what is now southern Scotland to his youngest brother, David. Alexander had no wish to lose control over so great a territory and sought to withhold it from his brother, for whom he evidently had no great love. David, however, was one of Henry I's favourites and, faced with the threat of English military intervention, Alexander was forced to yield. Despite the strain that this placed on their relationship, Alexander remained Henry's vassal and in 1114 led a force of warriors in Henry's campaign in Wales. It was also to England that Alexander turned for aid in resuming the reforms of the Scottish Church which his mother had initiated. Like Edgar he was a

16. St Andrews Cathedral, Fife. Alexander was determined that his bishops would not submit to an English metropolitan. The twelfth-century St Rule's Tower is the remaining portion of the early cathedral.

devotee of St Cuthbert – he was present at the translation of the saint's remains to a new shrine – and it was from Durham that he brought his candidate, Turgot, to fill the vacant bishopric of St Andrews, the spiritual head of his kingdom. Turgot's successor, Eadmer, came from Canterbury, and it was from the Yorkshire abbey of Nostel that Alexander secured the Augustinian canons to colonize his new foundation at Scone. Yet Alexander was far from being Henry's lapdog and he refused to permit either Turgot or Eadmer to profess obedience to the English archbishops, an act that would have underlined the subordination of the Scottish Church to the English. Correspondence with the papacy on this and other issues shows that Alexander was deeply concerned for the spiritual wellbeing of his kingdom.

Despite his dependence on England, the loss of control over southern Scotland made Alexander very much a man of Scotia. It was in the Gaelic heartland of his ancestral kingdom in Tayside that his power was based – he had held the earldom of Gowrie during Edgar's reign – and beyond churchmen, there is little evidence that he followed his brother's policy of settling Englishmen and Normans on

17. Alexander I's great seal image.

18. Scone Abbey, great seal showing the inauguration of a Scottish king.
Alexander I founded a priory of Augustinian canons at the ancient
inauguration site of the Scottish Kings (from a nineteenth-century facsimile).

his lands there. How he consolidated his hold over a territory that his predecessors had neglected is unknown, but the titles 'the Fierce' or 'the Strong' given to him by contemporary chronicles, and the comment that he 'held his kingdom with a great deal of effort', suggest that it was not an easy process. Nevertheless, the witnesses to his charters show that he could draw on the support of the leading Gaelic nobles and when he died in 1124 much of that support was bequeathed to his bastard son Malcolm.

5

DAVID I

(1124-1153)

By the natural order of things, David I should never have been king of Scots. The youngest son of Malcolm III and Margaret, he was aged about ten when he was driven into exile in England with his brothers and sisters following their parents' deaths in 1093. Although he may have participated in the campaign that placed his brother Edgar on the throne in 1097 – it was traditionally David's scheming that secured the blinding of his uncle, Domnall mac Donnchada – there was no place for him in the new order in Scotland and he remained in England. The marriage of his elder sister Edith to the new English king, Henry I, opened new career prospects for the young Scottish prince. Referred to as 'brother of the Queen' in English accounts and showered with his brother-in-law's patronage, David rose fast in Henry's service. As one of Henry's 'new men', David could expect rapid social advancement, and a steady stream of offices and lands flowed in his direction.

The first sign of significant change came in 1107 when David's brother Edgar died. David was now the probable heir of the new king, Alexander I. He was also a major landholder, for Edgar had bequeathed him rule over Cumbria, a territory that stretched from the northern end of Loch Lomond to the Solway in the south and eastwards into Tweeddale. Alexander was unwilling to hand over such a substantial portion of his kingdom, but threatened by Henry I's military interven-

19. David I from the initial letter M of Malcolm IV's great charter to Kelso Abbey (nineteenth-century facsimile).

tion he submitted by *c*.1113. Surrender, however, left a bitter taste in Alexander's mouth and relations with David were permanently soured.

David was now a great man, and his status was affirmed in 1113 when Henry arranged his marriage to Matilda de Senlis, the widowed countess of Northampton-Huntingdon. Although she was a widow with children, marriage to Matilda was a great honour for David. The daughter of Earl Waltheof of Northumbria and the Conqueror's niece Judith, she was of royal blood, lady in her own right of great estates and claimant to the forfeited earldom of Northumberland. David now became earl of Huntingdon as well as 'prince of the Cumbrian region', entering the topmost circle of the English nobility and securing the resources of one of the greatest magnate estates in England. Their only son, named Henry in honour of David's patron, was born *c*.1115. It was a mark of David's standing that his child was given precedence over Matilda's sons by her first marriage. The new man had arrived.

Until this point David had taken little interest in religious issues. His suddenly awakening religiosity may simply be a motif embellished by his biographer, Ælred of Rievaulx, to mark the transformation from dissolute youth to responsible adulthood, but it does appear that marriage and power marked a turning-point in David's life. David's

20. Drawing of one of the Lewis Chessmen found in 1831 on a beach in Lewis, in the Outer Hebrides. Made of walrus ivory they are thought to be of Anglo-Scandinavian origin and date from the twelfth century. They have been valued at over £500,000 each and only individual pieces from several sets have been found. It is assumed that more will surface in the future as the sets were probably buried complete for safe keeping.

mother, Margaret, and his aunt, Christina, abbess of Romsey, had had a powerful influence over his childhood, but it must be remembered that the English court was also awash with the repercussions of the religious reform that was sweeping western Christendom. In 1113, David showed his awareness of these developments when he founded an abbey at Selkirk in the heart of his Scottish lands. This was no mere act of an *arriviste* proclaiming his status through an example of conspicuous but conventional piety, for the monks chosen for the new community were Tironensians, members of a new and particularly austere order based at Tiron near Chartres. Through this act, bringing the first community of any of the reformed orders of monks into the British Isles, David proclaimed his support for the reform movement in general. He further underscored his devotion in 1116 when he attempted to visit St Bernard of Tiron in person, but the abbot died shortly before David arrived at the abbey. David's religious concerns, however, went far deeper and he also began the process of reforming the Church generally within his domain. His first act was to appoint his chaplain, John, as bishop of Glasgow, the spiritual overlord of the territories that made up Cumbria. Like his brother Alexander, despite his dependency on England, David was determined that his new

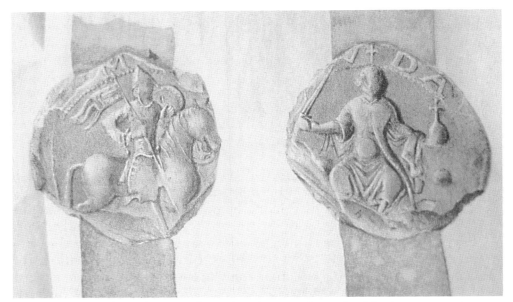

21. David I as king and warrior. Images from the king's great seal
(a nineteenth-century facsimile).

22. A silver penny of David I, minted from Cumbrian silver.

bishop should be free from the domination of the English Church. This determination opened a struggle that lasted for most of the twelfth century.

In 1124, already in what was for the medieval period his middle age, David succeeded to the Scottish throne. For most Scots, David was an unknown quantity and, for some, unwanted. Equally, for David, the Gaelic culture of his new kingdom was alien and barbaric. Indeed, the inauguration ritual, where the king was enthroned and acclaimed by his nobles with no Church involvement, far removed from the ecclesiastical ritual of English coronation, seemed so pagan to the devout David that he had a crisis of conscience over subjecting himself to it and needed to be persuaded to undergo the ceremony by his spiritual advisors. If this was not warning sign enough of where David's cultural preferences lay, the rapidity with which he began to introduce friends and dependents from England signalled a profound change in direction. There is little sign that David had introduced English colonists on to his lands in southern Scotland before 1124, but possibly as early as his inauguration at Scone he began to grant land to knights from the south, men on whom he came to rely for support and advice. One of the first beneficiaries was Robert de Brus, to whom the king granted Annandale. De Brus was followed by a small but influential group of men, often tenants from David's Huntingdon estates, such as Hugh de Morville and Robert Avenel, or associates such as Walter fitz Alan, the ancestor of the Stewarts. It is wrong, however, to think of David as flooding Scotland with colonists, for none of these men

23. Dryburgh Abbey, Borders, founded by Hugh de Morville, David's wealthy and powerful constable.

received lands north of the River Forth and there, in the heartland of his kingdom, David trusted in the loyalty of the great Gaelic lords, such as the earls of Fife and Strathearn.

The transition of power was always a dangerous time and for David it proved no less so. Early in 1125 a serious rebellion erupted in support of Alexander's bastard son Malcolm. Little is known of this man, who is not to be confused with another of the Canmores' political rivals, Malcolm MacHeth, who was active in the 1160s. It is clear, however, that he enjoyed widespread support within Scotland's Gaelic heartland, underscored by marriage to the sister of Somerled, lord of Argyll. The greatest challenge came in 1130 when, allied with Angus, earl of Moray, a descendant of King Lulach, Malcolm marched against David. At Stracathro, near Brechin in Angus, the rebels were crushed and Earl Angus killed, but Malcolm escaped to harass David for another four years until his capture and imprisonment in Roxburgh Castle. Victory was exploited ruthlessly, with David marching into Moray determined to impose his authority in the north. Angus's estates were seized by the king: the most important he kept for himself, establishing royal castles at places such as Elgin, Forres and Inverness as bases from which to consolidate his hold. To underpin his conquest,

24. Kinloss Abbey, Moray. This colony of Melrose monks provided David with a powerful agent in the newly conquered province.

25. Kelso Abbey, Borders. The first monastery of any of the reformed Benedictine orders founded in Britain.

he introduced colonists, most notably the Fleming Freskin, but also based his control of the region on alliance with native families, such as his kinsmen the earls of Atholl and Caithness. By the mid-1130s David had established his hold over most of mainland Scotland, extending the authority of the Scottish crown to its greatest reach yet and confirming his position as the second major power in the British Isles.

David's methods in Moray were characteristic of his policies throughout Scotland. The intrusion of colonists was balanced by a developing partnership with his Gaelic nobility and the retention of key estates as the foci for a network of new royal castles. In time, with David's encouragement, these castles attracted commercial settlements to which he granted charters of privileges – the origin of many of Scotland's royal burghs – thereby encouraging settlement of new colonies of traders and craftsmen to stimulate the economic development of his kingdom and establishing in the process outposts of royal power scattered throughout Scotland. The Church, too, was pivotal in this process. David carried through many of his brother's schemes, such as the reform of the bishopric of St Andrews – which he tried to have elevated to independent archiepiscopal status though in the end he had to content himself with only the consecration of his candidate as bishop, free from English overlordship – and in the course of his reign he was able to spread that process of reform to most of the mainland dioceses. The spread of the reformed monastic orders also continued apace. Soon after his succession to the throne he moved the monks from Selkirk to Kelso, in the shadow of his chief seat of power across the Tweed at Roxburgh. New Augustinian communities were established at Inchcolm and Holyrood, and in 1128 he re-founded Dunfermline as the royal abbey *par excellence*. Dunfermline participated in the royal expansion into Moray, receiving grants of estates and revenues from the king that formed the endowment of a new daughter house, Urquhart Priory. Founded in the heart of Earl Angus's former estate, the priory was a striking symbol of the extended reach of David's power.

26. The Tweed Valley from Wark Castle, Northumberland. David I's capture of this strategic fortress in 1136 secured his conquest of Northumberland.

27. Bamburgh Castle, the heart of Earl Henry's earldom of Northumberland.

The dramatic expansion of David's power down to the mid 1130s had been facilitated by his continuing friendship with Henry I. In the 1120s, the relationship was still primarily one of lord and vassal; indeed, in 1127 David was acting more as an English baron than a king in his own right when he was the first secular lord to swear the oath to uphold the rights of Henry I's daughter, Matilda, to succeed to the English throne should Henry produce no male heir. David's support for Henry in that issue, however, may have brought Henry's acquiescence or active support for David in securing the ecclesiastical freedom of Glasgow and St Andrews from the claims of York: the relationship clearly worked to the benefit of both parties.

On Henry I's death in December 1135 David could not prevent the disinheritance of Matilda in favour of the accession of her cousin's husband, Stephen. Within weeks, however, David had launched an invasion in support of his niece's claims, and also to take possession of those parts of northern England that he felt were his and his son's by right – Cumberland, Westmorland and the earldom of Northumberland. Attacking in the depths of winter, David captured Carlisle and Newcastle before settling down to besiege Durham, the fortress that had proved to be the bane of his grandfather, Duncan I. Swiftly assembling an army, Stephen marched to Durham's relief, but rather than give battle the two kings began lengthy negotiations that eventually produced a truce that greatly favoured the Scots. David, mindful of his 1127 oath, refused to perform homage to Stephen, but permitted his son to do so in order to gain control of the territory that Stephen was prepared to concede. Henry became earl of Huntingdon, was confirmed in possession of Carlisle and was granted the lordship of Doncaster. David surrendered Newcastle, but only on the understanding that Henry's rights to Northumberland be given justice in future. It was a shaky peace and nearly fell apart in 1137, but lasted until January 1138 when David launched his invasion of Northumberland. Although Stephen launched a counter-raid into Lothian in February, the initiative in the war lay with David. Scottish armies penetrated deep into England, one force commanded by David's nephew, William fitz Duncan, son of the short-reigned Duncan II, defeating an English army at Clitheroe in Lancashire. It was a brutal campaign of terror, marked by the widespread plundering and devastation of the countryside, the elimination of all resistance, and the driving off of female captives as slaves by David's Gaelic levies. Although David's biographers seek to excuse him for the atrocities committed, it is clear that the war was fought on David's terms and, although he tried to ensure the protection of Church property and the respecting of the sanctuary rights of those sheltering within churches, he accepted that 'collateral damage' was inevitable. It seemed that nothing could stop the Scottish juggernaut as it swept south towards York, but on 22 August at Cowton Moor near Northallerton his army was heavily defeated by a hastily assembled force under the nominal command of Archbishop Thurstan of York in a conflict known as the Battle of the Standard.

The Standard was a serious check to David's ambitions, but the spreading civil war in England between the supporters of Stephen and Matilda prevented Stephen from following up Thurstan's victory. As David consolidated his hold on the territory he had seized, Stephen was forced to come to terms. In early 1139, Stephen confirmed Earl Henry in possession of the estates granted to him in 1136 but also added Northumbria (excluding the castles of Newcastle and Bamburgh and the lands of the bishopric of Durham between the Tyne and Tees). While David handed over hostages to secure the peace, Earl Henry was further bound into Stephen's service by marriage to Ada de Warenne, sister of some of the king's key

28. Clitheroe Castle, Lancashire. Below its walls in June 1138, William fitz Duncan defeated an English army.

supporters. This time the peace seemed to hold, but in February 1141 Stephen was defeated and captured by Matilda's supporters at Lincoln and she prepared for her coronation at London. Suddenly recalling his oath to support Matilda's rights, David broke his truce with Stephen and marched south to join his niece for her coronation. At London, however, David and Matilda endured the humiliation of being driven from the city and only narrowly avoided capture at Winchester a few weeks later. Although David escaped, his experiences convinced him of the need for caution. After 1141, he concentrated on tightening his grip on the north of England, extending his hold over Durham, the north-western fringes of Yorkshire and at least northern Lancashire. Only in 1149 was a new offensive launched, partly as an inaugural raid by his great-nephew, Henry Plantagenet, the future Henry II, whom David had knighted at Carlisle. The aged David did not lead the offensive this time, command being entrusted to men such as William fitz Duncan. While the Scots once again came within an ace of seizing York, the campaign was at best a stalemate, so characteristic of the long civil war in England.

In contrast to war-ravaged southern England, after 1138 David's gains in the north appear as a haven of peace and prosperity. His secure hold on his enlarged kingdom enabled David to push ahead with the schemes for the development of his government, the modernization of the economy, and the reform and reconstruction of the Church, that he had set in motion soon after 1124. David continued to attract new men into his service, clerks and knights who formed the core of an evolving administration. For its structures, he drew on his early experiences in England, creating officers of state and developing a network of local administration on the English pattern. A chancellor, acting as the king's chief legal advisor, also controlled a writing office from which flowed an increasing tide of the parchment records of government: charters making or confirming grants of property and rights; letters to convey royal instructions to local officers; legal judgements in cases before the king's court; and records of royal revenues, rights and dues. The chamberlain controlled the king's finances, while the steward was responsible for the running of the household. The king's military affairs and the security of his household were overseen by the constable. Together with a host of lesser clerks and officials, these men transformed what had been a fairly small and informal royal household into an effective bureaucracy.

While war governed much of David's life down to 1141, he was more than simply a warlord. Influenced by English and Norman traditions, David projected an image of the king as lawgiver. Law codes attributed by tradition to David form the basis of medieval Scots law and the foundations of a system of sheriffdoms for the local administration of law were laid down by the king. But David was no remote figure, dispensing justice to only an exalted few, and the chroniclers make it clear that he saw it as his kingly duty to open the law to his subjects of all ranks. Ælred wrote of the king sitting at the door of his hall to receive petitions from the humblest of folk and even breaking off from his beloved hunting trips to hear the pleas of widows and the poor. To an extent it was a cultivated image, to be seen most clearly in the portrayal of David in the initial letter of his grandson's great charter to Kelso Abbey. There sits David, long-haired and bearded, presented as Solomon alongside the youthful and beardless Malcolm IV. The Biblical imagery, however, did not end with the wise lawgiver.

Amidst the planning for the war with Stephen, David found time to re-affirm his commitment to Church reform. Although he continued to patronize the established orders, such as the Benedictines and Tironensians, and founded one further Augustinian monastery at Cambuskenneth, most of his favour was targeted towards the new and even more austere Cistercian monks. In a society where austerity and simplicity were equated with piety and spirituality, the Cistercians were seen as enjoying a special closeness to God. For David, embarked as he was on a process of reform, and perhaps with his conscience pricked by the blood that he had spilled over the years, the prayers of these monks was welcome balm for his soul. In 1136, during the lull in his war with Stephen, he brought a colony of Cistercians from Rievaulx in Yorkshire to Melrose in Tweeddale. The colony prospered and in 1140, perhaps in atonement for the atrocities committed by their men in the 1138 campaign, David and his son, Earl Henry, founded an offshoot at Newbattle, followed in 1150 by two daughter-houses at Kinloss in Moray and Holmcultram in Cumberland. As his reign progressed, David may have felt ever more needful of Cistercian prayers.

All of this development was not achieved without cost. Over his reign, David devoted large sums to pious works, founding monasteries and building churches. Indeed, his fifteenth-century descendant, James I, looking at his seemingly prodigal alienation of crown resources to endow what seemed to him an ill-deserving Church, described him as 'ane sair sanct for the croune' (a sorry saint for the crown). Not only did he grant away portions of his land and revenue to the Church, however, but also used his resources to provide land to attract a colonizing aristocracy from England. Yet David clearly

29. Carlisle Castle, Cumbria. David I may have been the builder of the great twelfth-century keep that dominates the castle.

regarded his investments as money well spent. Indeed, the monks' policy of economic development of their estates, pioneering techniques in agriculture and stock-management, and the improved administrative methods brought by his colonial dependents, helped to kick-start Scotland's economy. Surpluses from monastic estates, especially wool and hides, stimulated the development of Scottish markets and overseas trade, channelled through David's chartered royal burghs. Growth was further stimulated by David's introduction of Scotland's first native coinage, minted with silver from the royal mines at Alston in Cumberland. In many ways it was on the back of this silver coinage that David's economic miracle was floated. Out of the profits of war, David built his new Scottish kingdom.

By 1150, David had drastically reshaped not only his own kingdom but also the balance of power within the British Isles. What historians term his 'Scoto-Northumbrian' realm, with its centre of gravity on a Roxburgh-Carlisle axis, was the dominant force in British politics, seen by southern English writers as a haven of good government in contrast to their war-torn homeland. The southern emphasis within his kingdom, however, should not obscure the fact that David was also a highly effective king of Gaelic Scotland. While there were many Gaels within Scotland who resented his anglicizing policies and personnel, the twenty years of stability that followed the capture of Malcolm in 1134 showed that he was accepted by and could count on the loyalty of most of the Gaelic nobility. Indeed, it has been said that David became more and more a Gaelic king as his reign progressed, successfully uniting the diverse components of his hybrid domain. The fact that David's extended kingdom proved transitory has led some to dismiss his achievement, but in the eyes of most contemporaries his greatness was unquestioned.

Despite his successes, for David the future held only uncertainty. In an attempt to secure his hold over his English gains, in 1149 when he knighted Henry Plantagenet he extracted a promise that the future king would respect the territorial *status quo*. A secure succession to the throne was an added safeguard and, in the person of Earl Henry, king-designate from possibly 1140 and an active colleague in government for his aged father, that seemed certain. In June 1152, however, aged about thirty-seven, Henry died. It was a devastating blow for David, who had never remarried after Queen Matilda's death in 1130 and who had no other adult son to whom the throne could pass. Now in his early seventies, David knew that he had to prepare for the future. In the summer of 1152, while he himself took Earl Henry's second son, the nine-year-old William, to Newcastle to receive the homage of the men of Northumberland, David sent his eldest grandson, Malcolm, on an arduous progress around Scotland in the company of Earl Duncan of Fife, to secure his recognition as king-designate. Still unsure as to whether he had done enough to secure the future of either his kingdom or his line, David died at Carlisle on 24 May 1153.

6

MALCOLM IV

(1153-1165)

Malcolm IV was barely twelve years old when his grandfather King David died. The succession of an untried boy opened the possibility of renewed challenges to the ruling line and, in a bid to limit the threat, Malcolm was inaugurated king at Scone within days of his grandfather's burial at Dunfermline. It was not enough, however, and rebellion swiftly erupted. In the west, Somerled and his nephews, the sons of the Malcolm imprisoned in 1134, moved to re-stake the claims of the mac Alexander lineage, and even in the heartland of the kingdom there were disturbances in support of the rival line. It was an inauspicious start.

By 1156 the domestic challenges were over: Somerled had gone in pursuit of a kingdom in the Isles for his son, Dubgall, and Donald mac Malcolm had been captured and imprisoned with his father in Roxburgh. A greater challenge, however, loomed on the horizon. In 1154, Malcolm's cousin Henry Plantagenet ascended the throne of England. Although he had promised in 1149 to respect the borders of the extended Scottish kingdom, in 1157 he laid claim to Cumberland and Northumberland. With England now united behind Henry the balance of power had swung decisively in his favour and Malcolm was in no position to resist. In return for the restoration of Huntingdon, Malcolm surrendered his grandfather's gains and became Henry's vassal. Further humiliation followed. Malcolm, despite his Gaelic

30. Malcolm IV from the initial letter M of his great charter to Kelso Abbey (nineteenth-century facsimile).

name – the last borne by any of Scotland's medieval rulers – had been brought up in the court of his anglicized father and exposed since early childhood to the chivalric ethos that permeated the noble elite of David's kingdom; for the teenage king, knighthood was the ultimate attainment. He had fully expected Henry to knight him but was rebuffed. A fresh opportunity to achieve knighthood came in 1159, however, when Henry summoned him as his vassal to give military service in his campaign against the Count of Toulouse. Probably against the advice of his leading nobles, who well understood the implications of Malcolm's readiness to accept the summons, Malcolm and his younger brother William embarked for France. On 30 June, at Périgueux, Henry at last knighted him. Although the campaign proved a failure, Malcolm had achieved one ambition.

Malcolm returned to Scotland to face the wrath of the Gaelic nobles who had supported him through the early years of his reign. Incensed by what they probably considered to be his wilful disregard of his kingly duties and by an act that might have compromised the independence of the kingdom, they attempted to seize him at Perth but were defeated and forced into submission. Malcolm immediately followed this success with an invasion of Galloway, whose ruler, Fergus, he defeated and forced into retirement as a canon in Holyrood Abbey, and which he then partitioned between Fergus's sons.

This forceful behaviour and love of military action stands in sharp contrast to the traditional image of Malcolm as weak and effeminate. This image has been reinforced by misunderstanding of his later nickname 'the Maiden', which reflected his personal celibacy and not his physical appearance or personality. Indeed, his celibacy was an extension of his devotion to his ideal of Christian knighthood, being modelled on the virginal purity of the ideal knight of Arthurian chivalric tradition, Galahad. It was, however, a cause for concern to those who wished to see the dynasty secured, especially after the first bout of illness that struck him in 1161, and his mother, Ada de Warenne, urged him to marry. Plans for his marriage to Constance of Brittany proved abortive, however, and after four years of recurring, serious illness he died at Jedburgh on 9 December 1165, still a virgin.

7

WILLIAM I

(1165-1214)

The succession to the throne of the twenty-two-year-old William heralded the opening of five decades of profound upheaval and change in the life of the kingdom. The longest reigning of Scotland's medieval monarchs, William presided over a period that saw unparalleled expansion in crown authority but also witnessed repeated challenges to that authority by pretenders from within the wider royal kin as well as the rigorous subjection of Scotland to the overlordship of the kings of England. The successes and failures of his long reign, however, should not detract from the personal achievements of one of Scotland's greatest rulers.

William was born probably in 1143, the second of Earl Henry's three sons by Ada de Warenne. On his father's death in 1152, William was taken by his grandfather to Newcastle and invested as earl of Northumberland. William, however, had little time to enjoy his patrimony, for in 1157 the surrender of the northern counties to the forceful Henry II disinherited the fourteen-year-old earl. Although Henry compensated him with Tynedale, the loss of the earldom embittered William, who spent twenty years trying to regain Northumberland. It became an ambition bordering on obsession and resulted in humiliation for both Scotland and her king.

Like his elder brother, William was a passionate devotee of the new chivalric ideal that was saturating European noble society. Equally deter-

31. William I as a mounted knight.

mined to win his spurs as a knight, William accompanied Malcolm on the Toulouse expedition of 1159 and was apparently knighted by his brother at Périgueux. On his return to Scotland he would have had the opportunity to indulge his teenage passion for warfare in the breaking of the protest of the rebel earls at Perth and the subsequent Galloway campaign. William's wholehearted embracing of the glamorous world of Frankish chivalry is underscored by references to him as 'William de Warenne', identifying him with his mother's kin, one of the great families of the Anglo-Norman elite, rather than with his father's royal Scottish ancestry. This apparent preference for all things Frankish was re-affirmed when a later chronicler observed that the Scottish kings considered themselves 'as Frenchmen in race, manners, language and culture; they keep only Frenchmen in their household and following and have reduced the Scots to utter servitude'. It was surely an exaggeration, but this casual remark emphasizes how far William had moved from his Gaelic roots.

A fortnight after the death of his brother, on 24 December 1165, William was inaugurated king at Scone. Almost immediately he used his new status in a bid to regain Northumberland. In August 1166 he met with Henry II in France and requested restoration, but was refused. Two years later, he approached Henry's rival Louis VII of France, seeking his diplomatic aid in the matter. It was a crassly provocative act which seriously damaged Anglo-Scottish relations and reduced Henry to such a fury that any mention of William threw him into a fit of rage. Once, he tore off his clothes and ripped the silk cover from the bed on which he was sitting before cramming his mouth with the straw that filled his mattress! It was hardly a promising start to their relationship.

Relations had improved sufficiently by April 1170 for William to attend Henry's court at Windsor and, using this as an opportunity to visit his Huntingdon estates, he remained in England until June for the coronation at Westminster of Henry's eldest son, also called Henry and known as the Young King to distinguish him from his father. On 15 June, William gave homage to the Young King, forming a personal bond that proved his undoing. In 1173, as the 'Angevin Empire' of Henry II slid into civil war between the old king on the one hand and his estranged wife, Queen Eleanor, the Young King and their ally Louis VII on the other, William was approached for aid by the rebels, who offered restoration of Northumberland. Against the advice of his counsellors but following the urging of a hawkish group of young household knights, William chose war.

In June 1174, following two inconclusive campaigns in 1173 and spring 1174, William again invaded England. Ill-prepared for the siege warfare necessary to take the castles that had been built in Northumberland since his grandfather's day, William made little headway. In early July he besieged Alnwick and dispersed most of his army on raiding missions throughout Northumberland. On 13 July,

32. Both sides of William I's seal.

caught unawares, William and the cream of his nobility were captured in a surprise attack. With his legs shackled beneath the belly of his horse, William was escorted south and consigned to prison at Falaise in Normandy. For Scotland, the humiliation had just begun.

To gain his release, William was forced to accept Henry's terms in what is known as the Treaty of Falaise. On 8 December 1174, having publicly acknowledged his subjection to Henry and promising hostages and the surrender of key fortresses in his kingdom, William was released. He confirmed the treaty on 10 August 1175 at York in a great ceremony where William publicly performed homage and fealty to Henry explicitly for his kingdom as well as his estates in England, promised to enforce the subjection of the Scottish Church to English jurisdiction, and 'ordered' his nobles and clergy to make their personal submissions to Henry. Unlike previous submissions, this treaty formally set out Scotland's vassal status, provided terms by which Henry could enforce compliance and established English garrisons in William's chief castles south of the Forth. Furthermore, it made clear that Henry considered the question of Northumberland and Cumberland firmly closed. Henry regularly reminded William of his status, especially by summoning him

33. Prudhoe Castle, Northumberland, besieged unsuccessfully by the Scots during their 1174 invasion of England.

34. Falaise, Calvados. William was imprisoned in the twelfth-century keep after his capture at Alnwick.

to court to explain his actions. He also chose to exercise his right as overlord to choose William's bride. By the 1180s and now in his early forties, William was still unmarried and, although he had fathered at least six bastards, his younger brother David was his only legitimate heir. He wanted a bride who would reflect his royal status and in 1185 requested Henry's permission to marry his overlord's granddaughter, Matilda, daughter of Henry the Lion, duke of Saxony. King Henry, however, had no wish to permit so politically significant a marriage to take place and instead offered him Ermengarde de Beaumont, the young daughter of the lesser nobleman Richard, vicomte of Beaumont sur Sarthe in Maine. William agreed reluctantly. Despite Henry's generous payment for the wedding celebrations – held at Woodstock on 5 September 1186 – and return of two of the forfeited castles as a wedding present, it was clear that the Scottish king felt slighted.

With southern expansion effectively shut off to him, William was forced to concentrate on domestic issues. More than one crisis faced him when he returned from Normandy. In Galloway, the sons of Fergus were in rebellion and had appealed to Henry II that he should take them under

35. Henry II, William's nemesis, doing penance at the shrine of Thomas Becket, stained glass panel in the Bodleian Library, Oxford.

his lordship. When one brother, Gillebrigde, had the other, Uhtred, murdered, Henry ordered William to bring the fratricide to justice, but Gillebrigde submitted to Henry and spent the next decade defying the powerless William. It was only in 1185 that William's protégé Roland, the son of Uhtred, took control of Galloway and restored it to a Scottish orbit. More serious was the rising in the north by Donald mac William, grandson of Duncan II, who took the opportunity of William's capture to claim the crown that he felt was rightfully his. Drawing widespread support, the rising rumbled on into the 1180s. In 1179, William, displaying the energy and dogged determination that was a hallmark of the central years of his reign, made the first of several expeditions into the north, extending direct royal power for the first time into Ross through the building of new castles on the north side of the Beauly and Cromarty firths. He failed, however, to bring Donald to battle and it was only in 1187 in a conflict near Garbh in Ross that the rebels were crushed, the pretender's severed head being brought to the king at Inverness.

This victory marked a new high point for royal power in the Highlands. Forced to look to the proper organization of royal government in the north, William radically overhauled the structures set in place by his brother and grandfather. The network of castles established as early as 1130 was strengthened and extended, as was the system of sheriffdoms based on them. In the 1190s, despite his faltering health, William again campaigned in the north, intent on humbling the perennial troublemaker Harald Maddadsson, earl of Orkney and Caithness. Royal armies reached the north coast at Thurso and Harald submitted, but it was not until after 1200 that he finally admitted the reality of William's power in the farthest reaches of Scotland. The Church, too, became a more effective bastion of royal power, with William appointing a loyal clerk to the key bishopric of Moray. But the most effective bulwark lay in the establishment of loyal knights in the region. The greatest beneficiary was his brother David, to whom he gave the strategic lordship of Garioch, which straddled the routes between Moray and the lowlands to the east, but the service of great Gaelic lords such as the earls of Fife and Strathearn was also rewarded by the granting of lordships in the central Highlands. Through achieving a balance between native and newcomer, William significantly tightened the royal grip on the north.

Amidst the crises that beset him from 1174 to 1187, William still found time for personal acts of devotion. His capture, which was attributed to the saintly intervention of the martyred archbishop of Canterbury, St Thomas à Becket, had affected him profoundly. In

36. Berwick Castle, Northumberland, one of the key fortresses William was required to surrender to Henry II under the terms of the Treaty of Falaise.

37. Arbroath Abbey, Angus, founded by William I and dedicated to St. Thomas of Canterbury, to whom he attributed his defeat and capture in 1174.

38. Seal of Arbroath Abbey, depicting the martyrdom of St Thomas of Canterbury, nineteenth-century facsimile.

honour of the saint, and no doubt to placate this holy defender of England's borders, in late 1178 William founded the great abbey of Arbroath and over the remainder of his reign endowed it with wide lands and revenues from the royal estates. This was the act of a deeply troubled soul.

The years of frustration and hard work after 1174 finally bore fruit in 1189 when Henry II, beset by his rebellious sons, finally proved mortal. The new king, Richard I, desperately in need of cash for his planned crusade, was prepared to negotiate with William. While again deferring a decision on Northumberland, Richard agreed to sell William back his freedom for the princely sum of 10,000 marks. On 5 December 1189, almost fifteen years to the day since his submission at Falaise, the so-called Quitclaim of Canterbury annulled the terms of the 1174 treaty.

William was now at the height of his power and concentrated on consolidating his hold over the kingdom. That he still hankered after Northumberland is clear: he sought to curry favour with Richard I by opposing his younger brother Count John's attempts to seize power in 1193 following the king's capture in Austria; by contributing 2,000

39. Drawing of the effigy of King John of England at Worcester Cathedral. John's threat of invasion forced William to come to terms, and on 7 August 1209, the Scottish king agreed to a humiliating treaty at Norham.

40. Norham Castle, Northumberland. Here, William and John negotiated the humiliating Anglo-Scottish treaty of 1209.

marks to Richard's ransom; and by arranging the marriage of two of his bastard daughters to important Northumbrian lords. It was all for nothing. When Richard agreed to sell the earldom to him in 1194 for 15,000 marks, it was on the condition that the chief castles remain in Richard's possession. It was, for William, an unacceptable condition and, bitterly disappointed, he returned to Scotland. But the matter did not end there. Later in 1194 William hatched a scheme, with Richard's agreement, for the marriage of his eldest legitimate daughter, Margaret, a child of no more than seven years, to Richard's nephew Otto, son of Henry of Saxony. William, who fell seriously ill in summer 1195, still lacked a male heir and, to the horror of his counsellors, attempted to have Otto recognized as his successor. Such was Richard's enthusiasm for the scheme that he agreed that Cumberland, Northumberland and Lothian would form Margaret and Otto's dowry. Just when it seemed that his life's ambition would be attained, however, William suddenly and for no clear reason backed out of the agreement. Yet he still sought an alternative settlement. In 1199, when John seized the throne of England, William used threats of military intervention in support of John's rival in a bid to extract concessions from the new king, but when

41. Chapterhouse ruins at Balmerino Abbey, Fife. Founded by
Ermengarde de Beaumont, wife of William I.

it came to the pitch his nerve broke and he disbanded his army. Fruitless negotiations dragged on leaving the festering issue unresolved.

William's increasing desperation over Northumberland was in part a response to his failing health and lack of a male heir. In April 1198, however, after twelve years of marriage, Queen Ermengarde at last gave birth to the son he craved. William was determined to pass to the child, Alexander, all that he considered to be the boy's birthright, and that included Northumberland. As the last years of William's life was to show, however, that was to be no easy task.

For William, the 1190s had been a veritable Indian summer. Freed from the shame of Falaise, it was in this period that the later reputation of the king had been made. To later generations of chroniclers, the bellicose and impetuous prince had been replaced by 'the Lion of justice', a style from which his most common modern title – William the Lion – is derived. To the chronically ill and ageing king, however, such high-blown titles would probably have held a bitter irony, for in the closing years of his life he watched much of the achievement of the 1180s and 1190s seemingly evaporate. It must have seemed a poisoned chalice that he was to pass to his son.

As had been the case throughout his life, the obsession with Northumberland contributed significantly to the dramatic reversal in his fortunes. William's attempts to ingratiate himself with Richard I in 1193 and refusal to immediately acknowledge John in 1199, both acts motivated by his determination to regain his lost patrimony, had soured his relationship with the youngest of Henry II's sons. Despite seven years of negotiations which produced a series of false dawns, by 1206 a solution was no closer and over the next three years the relationship between William and John descended into crisis as rumours reached the English king that William was again negotiating with his French enemies. In April 1209 William, again seriously ill, received the latest in a series of demands from John for a meeting in person. John came north with an army while William brought his forces to Roxburgh, and the two forces glowered at each other across the Tweed. Bowing to John's threats, William agreed to negotiate, but a return of his illness forced the suspension of talks and John returned south leaving his demands on the table. William's considered response infuriated John, who mustered for war, and, after considering armed resistance, the Scots caved in. On 7 August 1209, at Norham, William came to terms.

John's terms were a fresh personal humiliation for William. In return for a minor concession concerning the English castle at Tweedmouth, William was obliged to pay 15,000 marks to secure the peace, renounce his rights to the northern counties (which were to be given to Alexander to hold of the English crown when he came of age) give hostages as surety for payment and hand over his daughters, Margaret and Isabel, whose marriages John was free to arrange, possibly to his young sons, Henry and Richard. John's plan seems to have been that one of his sons would become the heir by marriage of William's heir, Alexander. Scotland's independence was not compromised on this occasion, but her aged king had been browbeaten and bullied into a one-sided treaty that promised much but had no real substance.

On top of this crisis came natural disaster. In September 1210 rainstorms swept Scotland, flattening much of the late harvest, and spate-filled rivers burst their banks. At Perth, William and his brother were almost trapped by floodwaters that swept away most of the royal castle but they escaped by boat. Then came disturbing news of threatened insurrection in the north which forced William to drag his weary bones to Moray. In January 1211, as William lay bed-ridden at Kintore, Gofraid mac William, son of the Donald killed in 1187, launched his bid for the throne. As the rising rumbled on into summer, the increasingly frail

42. Tomb effigy, believed to be that of William I, found in Arbroath Abbey.

William, his physician Master Martin bumping along in his baggage train, returned to the north and waged a futile three-month campaign. Leaving others to prosecute the war and fearful for the succession of his still underage son, William headed south with his family and sought a meeting with John in February 1212. Perhaps due to her husband's increasing physical incapacity, it is Queen Ermengarde who is credited with mediating a renegotiation of the 1209 treaty. The earlier terms were re-affirmed, but with the added provision that John would arrange Alexander's marriage – presumably to his infant daughter, Joanna – and that each king would come to the aid of the other. The treaty settled, the fourteen-year-old Alexander travelled south with John to be knighted at Westminster, presumably in anticipation of leading his first campaign against Gofraid. There was, however, to be no campaign in which Alexander could win his spurs, for by April 1212 the pretender had been betrayed and executed.

Entering his seventieth year, William, described as 'venerable' by one English clerk, was clearly preparing for his death. Queen Ermengarde, probably over twenty years younger than her husband, seems to have assumed some of his duties; she is found, for example, presiding jointly with the bishop of St Andrews over a complex court case. Alexander, too, was becoming more closely associated in affairs of state, being groomed for the office that his father expected soon to bequeath to him. Through 1213, William was setting his worldly affairs in order and was preparing for the afterlife, making new grants to churches and monasteries for his soul's ease and confirming his earlier gifts. But death did not come. In summer 1214, William made one last journey north to Moray to settle a new accord with John, earl of Orkney. It was an exhausting trip and as William made his slow progress south he was once more struck down by illness. On 8 September he reached Stirling, where his health continued slowly to decline. At last, on 4 December 1214, attended by his wife, son and brother, he died.

8

ALEXANDER II

(1214-1249)

On 5 December 1214, the day after his father's death at Stirling and five days before the old king's body was laid to rest before the high altar of his abbey at Arbroath, Alexander II was inaugurated at Scone. Four days of muted festivity followed, then on 9 December the new king met the funeral cortège as it crossed the bridge at Perth, escorted by the widowed Queen Ermengarde, and processed to Arbroath for William's funeral, Earl David presiding as his brother's chief mourner. Why the seemingly indecent haste? Why had the young prince to be made king before his father was even in his grave?

To the modern observer it perhaps appears obvious that Alexander, as the only legitimate son of William, would automatically have succeeded to the throne. But in 1214 male primogeniture – the succession of the eldest male offspring of the previous ruler – was still a recent innovation. It was sheer dynastic accident that the succession had passed through a direct line of descent from David I, not policy. In 1214, however, Earl David was the eldest male of the royal kin, and there was also the unresolved question of the Mac Williams, who clearly still enjoyed considerable support amongst segments of the Gaelic nobility. With Gofraid's rising still a recent memory, and Earl David such an unknown quantity to so many Scots, there was real fear of a challenge to Alexander's succession. Speed, therefore, was of the essence.

43. Alexander II enthroned in majesty, from his great seal.

44. Alexander II as an armoured knight on horseback, from his great seal.

The challenge was not slow in materializing. Within weeks of Alexander's inauguration the next Mac William claimant, Donald Bàn, had landed on the mainland and was raising rebellion in Ross and Moray. By mid-June 1215, however, the threat was over: Donald was dead and his head delivered to Alexander. The young king was no doubt relieved at the rapidity of Donald mac William's demise, for he had far bigger fish to fry. On the same day that Donald met his maker, hundreds of miles to the south King John was putting his seal to the Articles of the Barons. Among the concessions contained in the Articles, soon to emerge in fuller form in Magna Carta, was John's promise to do right by Alexander in respect of his sisters' marriages, the return of the hostages delivered up in 1209, and all unresolved questions relating to his liberties and rights. It is highly unlikely that Alexander had been ignorant of developments in England, for among the barons pressing their demands on John were his two brothers-in-law, Robert de Ros and Eustace de Vescy, while one of those on whose advice John accepted the demands was Alexander's constable, Alan, lord of Galloway. Although not yet seventeen, Alexander was already showing himself to be a shrewd political operator. After all, he had

45. Pluscarden Priory, Moray. Founded by Alexander II following the final defeat of the MacWilliams.

46. Site of Kincardine Castle, Aberdeenshire, where Alexander II received the severed heads of his defeated MacWilliam rivals.

been associated for two years in the running of the kingdom and had been exposed abruptly to John's duplicity and manipulation in 1212. He was clearly well informed of the deteriorating political situation in England and had no doubt used his time well in developing his inherited ties with John's disaffected northern barons, a group that included many men with personal kinship or tenurial bonds to the young king.

As England drifted into civil war in September 1215, Alexander prepared to capitalize on John's troubles. In October his army crossed the Tweed and he took the homage of the barons of Northumbria, apparently achieving in weeks what his father had failed to gain in fifty years. But John's men held the great fortresses of the region, and by the end of 1215 only Carlisle was in Alexander's possession. Soon, however, he was to reveal himself as John's equal in cynical manipulation and opportunism. In January 1216, as John moved against the northern rebels, the fearful barons turned to Alexander for aid. Revealing a skill in turning a favourable situation to his best advantage, he demanded and received their homage and fealty. John, however, was at his most dangerous when cornered and, swearing to 'make the fox-cub enter his lair' – no doubt a sneering reference to Alexander's red

47. Dumbarton Castle, Dumbartonshire. Alexander re-built the royal castle here and founded a burgh alongside it as a base for his campaigns into the Argyll and the Isles.

48. Playground of kings: The King's Deerpark in the hills overlooking
Kincardine, Aberdeenshire, was established as a hunting reserve
by the Canmore kings.

hair and youth – he led his army in an orgy of destruction through
south-east Scotland. Nothing was achieved by the slaughter, for
Alexander launched a counter-raid into Cumberland and in May, when
the French Dauphin Louis landed in Kent to take the English crown at
the request of the rebels, John's position in the north collapsed.

Alexander now established firm control of the northern counties.
On 8 August 1216, Carlisle again fell into his hands and became the
seat of a Scottish administration over Cumberland and Westmorland.
Indeed, the strength of his hold over the region and its effective incor-
poration into his kingdom has been recognized only recently, for, as
with earlier Scottish occupations of Carlisle, it proved impermanent.
In late summer 1216, however, Alexander seemed to hold all the aces.
Leaving Carlisle later in August, he crossed Stainmoor into Teesdale
and from there made an epic journey to meet with Louis at Dover.
Behind him, with the ferocity of a wounded tiger, John struck across
Alexander's lines of communication and once more threatened the
rebel position in the north. To protect his gains, Alexander hurried
northwards and had reached Scotland by the time John died at Newark
on 19 October. This event marked a decisive turning point in the war

and, although Alexander held on to his gains until December 1217, England rapidly reunited around the boy-king Henry III. Determined to pass John's territorial legacy intact to his son, the English regents dropped all reference to Alexander's grievances from the re-issued Magna Carta: for them this was non-negotiable until Henry came of age. Furthermore, Alexander now found himself excommunicated by the legate sent by the pope to safeguard Henry's heritage, and Scotland was placed under spiritual interdict. Bowing to the inevitable, in mid-December 1217 Alexander travelled to Northampton and gave homage to Henry for his English lands.

Displaying all his father's dogged determination, Alexander was intent that the effort and expenditure of the past years should not have been in vain. After two and a half years, negotiations dragged to a conclusion in June 1220. The settlement came nowhere near to meeting the broken promises of the 1209 and 1212 treaties. While Alexander was given the hand of one of Henry's sisters, Margaret and Isabel were only to be found 'suitable' but non-royal husbands in England before October 1221. Nowhere in the agreement was mention

49. Barnard Castle, County Durham. Alexander laid siege to the castle in 1216 as he marched south to join the French at Dover.

50. Dornoch Cathedral, Highland, built by Alexander's northern strongman, Gilbert de Moravia, bishop of Caithness.

51. Castle of Old Wick, Wick, Highland. Earl John of Caithness based his power on such fortresses.

made of the northern counties. Unlike his father, however, Alexander knew when it was time to back down and bide his time. He was young and the question of Northumbria could wait.

Like his father after 1174, Alexander now focused his attention on consolidating his power at home. Unlike William, however, he was no-one's vassal and was determined to remove any suggestion that his kingship was inferior in status to any in Europe, England in particular. The main stigma in this respect was the fact that Scotland's kings were inaugurated in a secular ceremony, not anointed and crowned in the ecclesiastical ritual common to England and France. In 1221, in the first move towards rectifying what he saw as a handicap, Alexander attempted to have the papal legate to Scotland anoint and crown him. The issue was referred to the pope who, under English pressure, rejected the move. On this point, however, Alexander was not simply going to let the matter drop and in 1233 made a second, equally unsuccessful bid. Further attempts may have followed, but it must have been clear to Alexander that the English, whose influence with the pope was almost always going to outweigh that of the Scots, would never willingly yield on the issue, despite the friendship between their kings. That friendship had been confirmed in June 1221 when Alexander married Henry's sister Joanna, a match that had first been proposed nineteen years earlier. It was, however, a sign of Scotland's improved standing, for while William had been forced to content himself with the daughter of a *vicomte*, his son had married a royal princess.

The next decade or so saw Alexander throw himself into the task of consolidating the authority that his father had struggled to impose over the remoter quarters of his kingdom. Long-running disputes, such as the rival claims to the earldom of Mar, were settled with firmness and justice, but it was in his dealings with potentially more explosive situations that he showed his true mettle. In early 1221, before his marriage, he led an army into the north-west Highlands and in summer 1221 and 1222 mounted naval campaigns in the west, targeted against the troublesome MacRuairidh kindred, descendants of Somerled, the twelfth-century ruler of Argyll, who had provided the Mac Williams with military aid. In autumn 1222, as Alexander prepared to go on pilgrimage to Canterbury, news came that the men of Caithness had murdered their bishop, Adam, the king's agent in the far north. Abandoning his plans, Alexander marched north and wreaked a savage justice on the perpetrators of this sacrilege in an unequivocal demonstration that the king's peace should run undisturbed and the royal will be unchallenged throughout his kingdom. Fresh disturbances in the north in 1228 were met and crushed with equal severity. The contrast with William's reign could not have been stronger.

52. Both sides of an Alexander II penny minted at Roxburgh.

53. Melrose Abbey, Borders. Alexander II promoted monks of Melrose as his agents.

While Alexander's ambitions in northern England may temporarily have been held in check, he expanded his authority in other directions. Plans to move westwards, into the area of nominal Norwegian sovereignty in the Isles, were driven by the awareness that it was from this quarter that much of the Mac Williams' mercenary aid had come. Alexander also wished to check the influence of the Uí Neill of west Ulster, also backers of the Mac Williams, who had been reasserting Irish power in the Hebrides. To this end, he encouraged the dreams of Alan of Galloway of building a kingdom in the Isles for his bastard son, cynically using his constable's ambitions to bring the crisis in the west to a head. A general war with Norway in 1231 was narrowly averted after one destructive Norse campaign in the Firth of Clyde area and Alan's schemes were halted abruptly, but not before the king had achieved his goal. In 1230, in a further rising, the Mac Williams were finally defeated and eliminated. In a pitiless display of royal justice, Alexander ordered the brutal 'execution' of the last Mac William, an infant girl whose brain was dashed out against the market cross shaft at Forfar. In 1235 it was the turn of Galloway. Determined to end the ambiguity of its relationship with the Scottish crown, Alexander imposed a partition of the lordship between the daughters of Alan, whose husbands were married to dependable Anglo-Scottish barons, crushing bloodily a rising in favour of their bastard brother. By 1236, Alexander was more surely master of the Scottish mainland than any of his predecessors.

It was from a position of some power that Alexander turned once again to the question of Anglo-Scottish relations. From 1234 he was again pressing for fulfilment of the 1209 treaty and, ignoring papal instructions to submit to Henry III, insisted on a final settlement. Rumours of war ran high in both kingdoms, perhaps encouraged by Alexander who knew exactly how the mind of his brother-in-law worked. Finally, on 25 September 1237 in a conference at York a treaty was settled that drew a line under the question of the northern counties and Alexander's long-standing personal grievances. In return for renouncing his claims to the counties and the 15,000 marks paid by his father to John, and abandoning the marriage arrangements for his sisters, Alexander received £200-worth of land in Cumberland and Northumberland with privileged jurisdiction over them. All copies of the 1209, 1212 and 1221 treaties were to be returned to the respective parties for destruction. At first sight, it appears that Alexander had caved in and yielded most of his claims in return for a relatively small return, but in the end it seems that Henry had recognized the dangers in permitting the uncertainty to drag on and Alexander had been bought off. It was not, however, a blueprint for peace and, after the death of Queen Joanna in 1238, Anglo-Scottish relations were tense, even coming to the verge of war in 1244.

Joanna's death presented Alexander with both a problem and an opportunity. With the death of Earl David in 1219 and his son, Earl John, in 1237, Alexander had no clear male heir. Joanna is a somewhat grey character, completely overshadowed by the dominating figure of the dowager queen, Ermengarde, who lived until 1234. Her inability to provide Alexander with any child, male or female, may be the reason why she failed to gain the place in her husband's counsels that Ermengarde held in William's. It also appears that, unlike his father's evident faithfulness to Ermengarde, Alexander had extramarital rela-tionships after his marriage to Joanna, perhaps an indication of the state of his relationship with her. It is possible that the pilgrimage to Canterbury that she began after the York meeting had been intended to secure saintly aid in the question of her fertility. At London, she was taken seriously ill and died there on 4 March 1238. A final sign of

54. Dunstaffnage Castle, Oban, Argyll, centre of MacDougall power.

Alexander's indifference towards his wife might be marked by his failure to bring her remains north for burial. Instead she was buried in the Cistercian nunnery of Tarrant Kaines in Dorset, a community with which her husband had no previous relationship. While the problem of an heir seems to have been resolved temporarily by the tacit recognition of his cousin Robert de Brus, lord of Annandale, as heir presumptive, Alexander quickly set about finding a wife. This task also provided him with the opportunity to underscore his independence of England, a point reinforced in May 1239 when he married Marie de Coucy, the daughter of a powerful French baron. At last, on 4 September 1241, she gave birth to their only child, a son. He was not named William in honour of his grandfather, nor even David in memory of the founder of the royal line, but Alexander, and perhaps in this we come closest to glimpsing the hidden personality of his father.

55. Melrose Abbey, Borders. Alexander II's body was interred before the high altar in 1249.

King Alexander emerges as a highly complex character. His ambition was matched by an energy, ability and ruthlessness that was closer to that of his great-grandfather than his father. Unlike his father, too, he possessed a pragmatic realism that perhaps saved him from the humiliation of a second Falaise for Scotland. In his religion, he was the greatest patron and founder of monasteries since David I. He supported conventional monasticism, co-founding a Cistercian abbey with his mother at Balmerino in Fife, and showering Melrose with favour, while his special foundation was Pluscarden in Moray, a colony of the new and especially austere Valliscaulian order of monks. Pluscarden was founded *c*.1231, perhaps as a thanks-offering for his final elimination of the Mac Williams and as a means of salving his conscience for the brutality with which that end was achieved. He was also, however, a supporter of the new orders of friars, especially the

56. Another of the beautiful Hebridean chesspieces from the beach on Lewis.

Dominicans, whom he invited to Scotland in 1230 and provided with their first convent at Edinburgh. In doing so he was signalling an awareness of and support for the new and still controversial spiritual developments within the Church, something that suggests that his religious patronage went beyond the conventional or traditional pious behaviour of the ruling elites. But, while he clearly supported the processes of internal reform within the regular clergy, he routinely exploited his influence over the Church to provide additional support for his authority. For example, monks from Melrose, his favoured monastery, were appointed bishops in the politically sensitive dioceses of Caithness, Ross and Whithorn, and in Galloway the native heads of the local Cistercian houses were deposed in favour of Melrose monks after Alexander suppressed the 1235 rebellion there. For Alexander, religious patronage and personal piety may have been investments to be cashed in for political considerations.

Royal control over the Church was just one manifestation of Alexander II's firm grip on the political life of his kingdom. The political elite, too, was tightly controlled through a mixture of coercion and patronage. Crown-magnate tensions were not unknown, as in 1242 in a brief crisis which followed the death in suspicious circumstances of the heir to the earldom of Atholl, when a majority of the nobility forced the king to take firm action against the family suspected of his murder, who were currently riding high in his favour. Otherwise, magnate ambitions were harnessed to the needs of the crown, and this can be seen most clearly in the military operations that punctuated his reign. Support for Alexander's military objectives brought tangible rewards in the form of land and office, illustrated most spectacularly by the rise of Farquhar MacTaggart from obscurity to the earldom of Ross. This co-operation between crown and nobility, clear testimony of Alexander's rapport with his lords, served to underpin the consolidation of royal authority in the northern and western mainland, regions where control had been intermittent during his father's reign.

By the 1240s, Alexander's authority within Scotland had reached its zenith. On the mainland, only the MacDougall lordship of Lorn had an ambiguous relationship with the crown, and beyond it beckoned the Hebrides. For Alexander, the Isles represented both unfinished business and a continuing challenge, for so long as they remained outwith Scottish sovereignty they posed a potential threat to the security of the kingdom. In 1244, Alexander offered to buy the Isles from Norway, an offer rejected out of hand by the Norwegian king,

Håkon IV, who similarly dismissed subsequent offers. Suspicions that the MacDougalls, who were vassals of both kings, were also involved in negotiations with Henry III, prompted Alexander to end the ambiguity for once and for all. In the summer of 1249 a major royal naval expedition cruised the waters of the Inner Hebrides. In early July, it anchored off the island of Kerrera in Oban Bay, poised to strike against the heart of MacDougall power. On 8 July, at the height of his power, Alexander II died suddenly in his tent on Kerrera, struck down, it was rumoured, by the power of St Columba, protector of the Isles.

9

ALEXANDER III

(1249-1286)

Few kings anywhere, let alone Scotland, have enjoyed for so long a positive reputation such as that of Alexander III. Remembered in tradition as the king of Scotland's 'Golden Age', he has in the past been presented as the ideal monarch who brought the realm to the peak of its medieval prestige, power and prosperity, presiding over a united kingdom in which an incipient sense of nationhood was taking root. Only recently has that view come to be challenged, with the king presented instead as a 'lucky mediocrity' whose reputation was created after his death as part of a propaganda offensive mounted by the Bruce and Stewart kings to establish their legitimacy. For writers medieval and modern, however, what has always been most important about Alexander III is the myth rather than the man. Like all icons, it is probably the aspirations invested in and the dreams symbolized by the king that have ensured his immortality rather than his personal achievements or character. But there must surely have been some substance upon which to build the myth?

Alexander III's reign did not begin auspiciously. Only five days after his father's death and before the old king's burial at Melrose, the eight-year-old Alexander was brought to Scone for his inauguration. There was immediate controversy over procedures, for Alan Durward, justiciar of Scotia and husband of the new king's bastard sister Margaret, urged that

57. Peel Ring of Lumphanan, Aberdeenshire, one of the castles of the ambitious Alan Durward.

Alexander should be knighted before he was inaugurated. Following recent English precedent, the man who knighted the king would most probably become his regent, and it is likely that Durward was aspiring to do so. Walter Comyn, earl of Menteith, head of the powerful Comyn family and Durward's chief political rival, argued strongly and successfully against the knighting. The ceremony proceeded in its traditional form of enthronement, acclamation and declaration of the king's lineage by a Gaelic *seannachaidh*, although the Scots were soon lobbying at Rome again in an attempt to secure the rights of coronation and unction. Menteith had won on this occasion, but Durward continued to hold the political leadership of the administration and his supporters filled the key offices of state. There were some shows of unity, however: in June 1250 the young king, Queen Marie and the leading clergy and nobles assembled at Dunfermline for the translation of the remains of Malcolm III's wife, Queen Margaret, to a more splendid shrine to mark her canonization by the pope. Durward, however, was manoeuvring to increase his authority, and he appears to have succeeded in combining the justiciar-ships of Scotia and Lothian, the two key judicial and administrative offices, into a single justiciarate in his possession.

Durward's star seemed to be in the ascendant. In summer 1251 plans for a continuation of good Anglo-Scottish relations through the marriage of Alexander to Margaret, daughter of Henry III, were finalized. On Christmas Day 1251, at York, Henry knighted his future son-in-law, and on the following day the young couple were married. Alexander then gave homage for his English lands and, probably well schooled by his advisors, rejected an English attempt to extract his homage for Scotland too. What followed, however, pulled the carpet from under Durward's feet. Alexander, or more likely Henry acting in his name, demanded the resignation of all the Scottish royal officials present. It soon became clear that Durward's opponents, by presenting him as a threat to Alexander and Margaret, had succeeded in calling on Henry to aid them in prising

58. Remains of the Shrine of St Margaret, Dunfermline, Fife. Alexander attended the translation of his newly canonized ancestress's relics to their new shrine in June 1251.

59. Both sides of Alexander III's seal.

power from their rival. Durward, indeed, may have played into their hands by attempting to secure the legitimizing of his wife at Rome, for this would have made her and his daughters Alexander's nearest heirs. Rumours were certainly circulating that he had planned to murder the young king and take the throne for himself.

In place of Durward stepped Menteith and a government composed largely of the Comyn family and their associates. The young Queen Margaret, who comes across from her letters as spoiled and wilful, resented their control over her, and wrote at length to her father to complain. He, however, was preoccupied with problems in Aquitaine, and when he wrote to the Scots it was to seek military aid. Few responded to his request but one who did was Alan Durward, who in 1254 travelled to Burgos in Castile with Margaret's brother, the future Edward I. Soon, Durward was riding high in Henry III's favour and turning the king's mind against those who had toppled him from power. Menteith and his allies, however, had also alienated much of their support in Scotland. In July 1255, two English emissaries managed to speak privately with Alexander and Margaret and reported back to Henry with an unhappy tale of mismanagement and mistreatment. Moving quickly north, Henry made contact with leading Scottish opponents of the Comyns identified by Alexander and Margaret, amongst them Durward. In August 1255, Durward and the earl of Dunbar staged a coup, seizing Edinburgh Castle and with it control of the king. Protracted negotiations involving Henry III, Alexander III and the two noble factions followed, but in September, when the Comyns rejected all proposals, Alexander and Henry established a government of their choosing with a term of office to expire on Alexander's twenty-first birthday in 1262. It lasted barely two years.

The 1255 settlement fell, like its predecessor, to a coup. Throughout 1257, attempts at conciliation between the government and the Comyn faction had been underway but no headway was made. In a night time raid in late October, Menteith and his allies kidnapped the king at Kinross and the government disintegrated in confusion. Growing political crisis in England prevented Henry from making more than a token intervention before January 1258, but by that date it appears that the Comyns had already lost control of an increasingly self-confident Alexander, who summoned a parliament to meet at Stirling in mid-April. A settlement was hard to find, but by September 1258 the opposing factions had been hammered into a lop-sided union in which the Comyns were the dominant force. The years of crisis were now over, and for the remainder of the period until Alexander took personal control of his government in 1260, unity was restored to Scotland.

60. Both sides of an Alexander III coin.

While Alexander's assumption of personal rule brought an end to the eleven years of political division in Scotland, the portents did not seem to augur well. The year 1260 was one of famine and foul weather. Food shortages saw the price of flour rocket, while a wet autumn brought another spoiled harvest and the promise of dearth to come. While Nature may have frowned, the world of politics, however, seemed to smile on Alexander. His ending of the arrangements for his minority government had brought no response from his father-in-law, who was pre-occupied with a mounting crisis at home. It was perhaps in full knowledge of Henry III's weakness that Alexander and the heavily pregnant Margaret travelled to England. Alexander demanded payment of Margaret's dowry, now nearly ten years in arrears, and it was rumoured that he had even gone so far as to suggest that, since Henry had not honoured his obligations under the 1237 York agreement, the issue of his claim to Northumberland should be reopened. It has been said that the 1260 visit brought a renewal of the friendly relations that had existed between the kingdoms before 1249, but more exactly it brought a return to the balance in the relationship that Alexander II had achieved. Having secured Henry's renewed promises concerning the dowry, Alexander returned to Scotland leaving Margaret behind in England for the birth of his first child (a daughter, Margaret, born in February 1261) – much to the concern of his councillors – but only once he had secured guarantees of their safe return. Arrangements, too, were made for the setting up of a

61. Bishop's Palace, Kirkwall, Orkney. Håkon IV retreated here after his defeat at Largs and died in the palace in December 1263.

62. A sixteenth-century depiction of the parliament supposedly held in the 1270s with Alexander III and Llewelyn, Prince of Wales sitting at the feet of Edward I.

minority council should he die before Margaret and the child returned to Scotland. At least some of the lessons of 1249-58 had been learned.

Alexander returned to his kingdom seemingly intent on finishing the uncompleted business of his father's reign. The question of the Isles had fallen somewhat into abeyance during the minority, Ewen MacDougall of Lorn having come into the Scottish king's peace and been restored to his lands in 1255. But despite growing Scottish influence in the west, this was still notionally Norwegian territory and a source of potential danger to Scottish security. In 1261, Alexander tried a return to his father's original policy of seeking a diplomatic solution and sent an embassy to Bergen to negotiate with King Håkon IV. Having spent his reign in asserting rigorous royal power throughout his domain, Håkon was in no mood to permit any diminution in his authority and refused to bargain. The Scottish embassy was even detained over winter in Norway when it tried to leave without the king's formal permission. The diplomatic route having failed, Alexander turned to warfare.

63. Largs, Ayrshire. Monument to the battle of Largs, the last significant conflict in the Scottish-Norwegian struggle for mastery of the Hebrides.

In 1262, Alexander started to apply pressure to the Islesmen. Instead of submitting, however, they sent frantic messages to Håkon, who in 1263 gathered a fleet with the aim of reasserting Norwegian authority in the west. On 11 July 1263 the fleet sailed west, very late in the year for a campaign in the uncertain waters of the Hebrides. Throughout the summer, Alexander had been making preparations for the coming storm, ordering the repair and strengthening of royal castles on both the east and west coasts – for no-one knew where the Norwegians might strike – and instructing local military levies to be held in a state of readiness. On 10 August, Håkon left Orkney for the Hebrides, already aware that his support amongst the Islesmen was draining away. In early September, after plundering their way south and round Kintyre, the Norwegians entered the Firth of Clyde.

Alexander had made his headquarters at Ayr and from there he spun out the negotiations that Håkon now sought. The Norwegians might, militarily, have had the upper hand, but time was on the Scots' side, for Alexander knew that Håkon would have to withdraw soon to a secure winter base. In an attempt to force the Scots into a more pliant mood, Håkon sent part of his fleet up Loch Long, where it was hauled across the porterage at Tarbet and launched on Loch Lomond to spread terror throughout Lennox and Menteith. The Scots, however, bided their time. Towards the end of September, Håkon moved the main body of his fleet across the firth to an anchorage between the island of Little Cumbrae and the mainland at Largs, perhaps in preparation for a landing on the Cunningham coast. On 30 September, the first of the equinoctial gales struck and the following morning found three Norwegian galleys and a merchantman beached on the shore at Largs. Throughout the day, small groups of locals and Norwegians skirmished around the ships, then on 2 October, Håkon himself landed with a select force to salvage what he could from the wrecks. The scene was now set for what has been described variously as the defining moment in the making of the medieval Scottish state, a battle of epic proportions, or an insignificant brawl on an Ayrshire beach.

Stripping away the myth from the facts, the 'battle' of Largs emerges as an inconclusive skirmish between two small forces. Håkon had wisely returned to his ships when the Scots appeared, leaving experienced commanders to stage a planned withdrawal in the face of what was at first assumed to be the main Scottish army led by Alexander himself. An Alexander did indeed command the approaching force, but it was not the king but Alexander Stewart, the most powerful Scottish noble in the west, whose lands in Bute and Cowal had been ravaged by

64. Crail Kirk, Fife. The thirteenth-century parish church, built by the affluent burgesses of Crail, reflects the trading wealth of Alexander III's Scotland.

the Norwegians. A running skirmish ebbed and flowed over the shingle banks around the mouth of the Gogo Water, but the Scots were unable to force a more general battle and the Norwegians returned to their ships. Håkon, whose fleet was now running short of supplies, was forced to face reality and on 5 October began to withdraw northwards, reaching Orkney on 29 October. He chose to over-winter there, taking over the bishop's palace in Kirkwall. In November, the king's health began to deteriorate and on 16 December he died.

Håkon's death removed what was still a formidable opponent for Alexander. Certainly, the western expedition of 1263 had been a failure by anyone's standards, but Håkon had shown the vulnerability of the Scottish mainland to sea-borne raiders and had returned to Orkney with most of his fleet and army intact. His son, King Magnus, however, had many problems stored up from his father's reign to contend with at home, and was in no position to prosecute the war. From a position of strength, the Norwegians now found themselves on the defensive. Alexander chose now to flex his muscles. An embassy in spring 1264 was sent packing, but messengers in the autumn were told that negotiations could start the following summer: Alexander was not going to be diverted from his prey. In summer 1264 he gathered a fleet in Galloway to invade Man, whose king, Magnus Olafsson, only averted invasion by travelling to Scotland to submit personally to Alexander. When the Manx king died the following year, Alexander annexed his kingdom to the Scottish crown. Part of the Scottish fleet from Galloway turned instead into the Isles, where it received the submission of many of the chieftains who had sided with Håkon the previous year, while a land campaign punished those in Caithness and Ross who had submitted to the Norwegians. By the time the Norwegian envoys arrived in 1265, Alexander had imposed his lordship over most of the Isles; a negotiated settlement was little more than a formalizing of established fact.

The terms of the Treaty of Perth of 1266, by which lordship over the Isles was transferred from Norway to Scotland, show that Alexander was prepared to make concessions to ensure that his possession was secure. In return for a single payment of 4,000 marks, to be paid in

65. A coin of Alexander III's reign.

four annual instalments, and an annual tribute of 100 marks in perpetuity, Man and the Isles became part of the kingdom of the Scots. The former island kingdom was intended to become the appanage of the Scottish heir apparent, Alexander, who had been born in January 1264, but it was to be controlled until his adulthood by a series of crown bailies. The significance of Alexander's achievement in gaining the Isles has often been overlooked, for the chief prize, Man, was to remain in Scottish hands for only thirty years. By annexing the former kingdom of the Isles to his own kingdom, Alexander had extended his power dramatically, pushing his influence south into the Irish Sea and west into the Gaelic world of north-western Ireland and the Hebrides. It represented a significant shift in the balance of power between Scotland and England in the region, which Henry III, a prisoner in the hands of his own nobles, had been incapable of preventing. Until James III added control of Orkney and Shetland to the Scottish crown in the 1460s, it took Scotland to its greatest medieval extent. The apparent ease of the Scottish takeover, however, was deceptive, for in 1275 Alexander was forced to send an army from Galloway against Gofraid Magnusson, illegitimate son of the last Manx king, who had seized control of the island and proclaimed himself king. Scottish control was reimposed in a tide of blood and steel, but it is clear that although they had been bludgeoned into submission, the Manx were still not reconciled to their new masters.

The Treaty of Perth ended a war and transferred what had become effectively only a nominal overlordship from the Norwegians to the Scots. It did not bring an immediate return to friendly relations between the two kingdoms. Norway, though, was a declining power in the later thirteenth century and, with the succession of the young teenage Eric II Magnusson in 1280, it seemed likely to remain weak until its new king was old enough to make his mark. For the Norwegians in the 1280s, good relations with their North Sea neighbours were an imperative and treaties were sought with both England and Scotland. In September 1281, the Scoto-Norwegian treaty was sealed with the marriage in Bergen of the thirteen-year-old Eric to Alexander's only daughter, the twenty-year-old Margaret. Although the marriage alliance cost the Scots heavily – Alexander promised 14,000 marks and resumption of the 'annual' due for the Isles – it ended the tension that had lingered between the kingdoms since the 1260s. Much hope was placed in the match, but in April 1283 Alexander received the news that his daughter had died shortly after giving birth to his granddaughter, to whom the name Margaret had also been given. It was just the latest in a string of blows to rain down on the king.

The first of these blows had fallen in February 1275 when Queen Margaret died at Cupar in Fife. We have no clear image of Alexander's relationship with his wife, but later tradition speaks of it in terms of warmth, closeness and affection, painting the king as a devoted husband and father. Certainly, Alexander, who was still a young man in 1275, showed no inclination to remarry, and it was only in 1285, with the succession in question, that he bowed to political pressure on that front. Five years after the queen's death the second blow fell and Alexander returned to Dunfermline for the funeral of his younger son, the seven-year-old David. Then came Margaret's death in Norway, the blow softened by news of the birth of his first grandchild. All Alexander's hopes now lay with his surviving son, Alexander, a healthy and newly-married young man of nineteen. Young Alexander had been married in November 1282 to Margaret, daughter of Guy de Dampierre, count of Flanders, thereby strengthening Scotland's ties with one of its most important continental trading partners. Like the Norwegian marriage of his sister, it was a match of great significance and marked Scotland's re-emergence onto the European stage. Like Margaret's, however, it was ill starred. In January 1284, the king was in Dunfermline again, burying the last of his children. Politics now overrode sentiment, for Alexander's only living legitimate heir was his nine-month-old granddaughter in Norway. It was imperative that the king should re-marry.

In February 1285, having taken counsel from his advisors, Alexander sent a high-powered delegation to France to seek a bride for him. They returned with the offer of Yolande, sister of Jean, count of Dreux, and in October 1285 she arrived in Scotland. The marriage was held with great splendour at Jedburgh, but later chroniclers, wise after the event, described how the lavish feast was marred by the sudden appearance of a ghostly apparition amongst the revellers. Few could have foretold its message. On 19 March 1286, Alexander was in Edinburgh holding a council with his nobles that seems to have stretched into a long, wine-lubricated 'business lunch'. Late in the afternoon, he decided to return to Yolande, who may have been pregnant, and who was currently residing at the royal manor of Kinghorn in Fife. Against the advice of the ferryman, he crossed the Forth in deepening darkness and in the teeth of a gathering storm. At Inverkeithing, the bailie tried to persuaded him to stay in his house overnight, but the king was determined to complete the

66. Jedburgh Abbey, Borders, where Alexander celebrated his marriage to his second wife, Yolande de Dreux, in October 1285.

eight miles remaining of his journey and rode off into the night, soon to become separated from his companions. It was the last time he was seen alive. The following morning, Alexander's body was found lying on the foreshore at Pettycur, less than one mile from his destination. Modern tradition would have it that he rode to his death over the cliffs in the darkness, but the contemporary records are less dramatic. Galloping along the track that followed the beach at the foot of the cliffs, his horse had stumbled in the sand and thrown him, breaking his neck in the fall. Scotland held its breath, all eyes on Yolande, who claimed to be with child. If she gave birth to a son, then, although there would be the inevitable long and probably troubled minority, there would at least be security and certainty for the future. Even a daughter would be preferable to a granddaughter in distant Norway. By late summer Yolande had either miscarried or had lied about her pregnancy. There was to be no male heir for the Canmore line.

As a model king, Alexander III is, at first glance, a rather odd choice. Succeeding to the throne as a boy of eight, for the first decade of his reign he was little more than a cipher in the hands of competing noble factions. Asserting his own personal authority, however, he brought the divisions to an end and united the nobility once more behind the monarchy. In a brief demonstration of royal ruthlessness, he concluded the long process of extending Scottish control over the Isles, and showed that he was willing and capable of using overwhelming force to cow dissent amongst his new subjects. War and the rewards of victory served to further unite the nobility behind him, with former rivals from his minority years serving alongside each other in the campaigns of 1262-65 in the north and west. Pragmatism, however, made Alexander realize that he was likely to stand a better chance of securing his grip on the Isles through a negotiated settlement and the Treaty of Perth offered the Norwegians a face-saving exercise that brought some profit from the military failure of 1263. He well understood that Norway, even in decline, was a potent power in the northern world, and the marriage treaty of 1281 marked the normalization of Scoto-Norwegian relations after years of strain. This much is positive and self-evident, but what of the later traditions of his reign as a time of peace, abundant harvests and prosperity?

It is a historical fact that the late thirteenth century in Europe generally was a time of expanding markets, rising population and stability. The picture was not entirely rosy, the beginning of Alexander's personal rule, for example, coinciding with a succession of poor harvests and resultant famine and price inflation. Nevertheless, it is clear that the Scottish economy was expanding rapidly during Alexander's reign, with Berwick emerging as one of the most important ports in the northern sector of the North Sea and the major conduit through which Scottish produce, especially wool, woolfells and hides, flowed in to the expanding European market. The expansion of Scotland's trade brought a net inflow of silver to the kingdom, bringing a time of boom that is most clearly marked in the building programmes undertaken by the major monastic landlords and great nobles, who flaunted their wealth in public display. At monasteries and cathedrals from Dundrennan in Galloway to Dornoch in Sutherland, and castles such as Bothwell, Caerlaverock or Kildrummy, new building marks the prosperity that Alexander's peace fostered. But was this prosperity Alexander's personal achievement, or was he just the lucky beneficiary of the good times for all throughout western Europe?

There is no simple answer to that question. Certainly, Scotland cannot but have benefited from the growing prosperity of Europe and,

67. Edward I as depicted by Matthew Paris at his coronation.

with her established trading links, was well placed to cash in on the demand for her raw and semi-finished produce. But trade does not flourish in uncertain times and the stability of Scotland after 1265 was clearly a major boost. Alexander may have been lucky in that his war was short and geographically remote from the economic heart of his kingdom, and that both the political situation in England during the 1260s and his good family relationship with the Plantagenets in the 1270s and 1280s ensured lasting stability on his only land frontier. That is not to say that the relationship was not, at times, strained, but Alexander was always secure enough at home to be able to face down the pretensions of his neighbour. In 1275, for example, when he came to Westminster for the coronation of his brother-in-law, Edward I, it was only with written safeguards that his visit was not a sign of subservience. Similarly, when he gave his homage for his English lands it was made explicit that his submission was for those and those alone, not for Scotland. His conduct of diplomacy and politics, then, seems to be that of a capable man, not the lucky mediocrity of recent tradition. But his achievement in these areas is unremarkable, certainly in comparison to either David I or Alexander II. So why did he become such an icon of the kingly ideal for later generations of Scots?

68. Pettycur, Kinghorn, Fife. The nineteenth-century monument stands above the foreshore where Alexander III's body was found on March 1286.

Two main factors appear to have been behind Alexander's later reputation. The first lay in the needs of the Bruce and early Stewart kings to establish their legitimacy as Scotland's rightful rulers in the face of challenge from the Balliol family and the English crown. Their propaganda saw Alexander III's reign presented as a time when the land flowed with milk and honey, when Scotland was safe, secure and powerful, blessed by God. Their purpose was to paint what came after as a time of darkness and despair, when the country turned from the path of righteousness and chose as its king a man who was not its rightful ruler. God turned his back on Scotland, and blighted the realm with war, defeat and dishonour until the Scots recognized their error and turned instead to their rightful king, Robert Bruce. He was portrayed as the man who inherited Alexander III's legacy and restored the land to the freedom and prosperity that it had enjoyed under its last legitimate king. So, Alexander's reputation was enhanced to make what fell between his reign and that of Good King Robert seem blacker still. The second strand, too, had more to do with a later period than with Alexander's own lifetime, for he was taken up as a model of good kingship in the later fourteenth and earlier fifteenth century by chroniclers who were seeking to stress the benefits of powerful royal government. For them, who lived in a time when some nobles were considered 'over mighty', Alexander, who endured a faction-ridden minority where rival bands of nobles contended for power, but who asserted his own authority over them and harnessed their ambitions to his own ends, was the perfect ruler. Furthermore, not only had he checked noble ambitions, he had projected Scotland's power abroad, defeating the Norwegians and rebuffing English pretensions. Under his firm rule, Scotland had emerged as a recognizable nation. To these later chroniclers, the prosperity of his reign was the reward for strong monarchical rule and was an objective towards which his successors should strive. For them, too, the Golden Age idea became a powerful image of what had been lost through the weakness of Scotland's contemporary rulers.

So, does Alexander III deserve his golden reputation? There is no quick or easy solution to that question, but the answer should probably be a qualified 'No'. He was a successful ruler who governed a stable and peaceful realm, where the nobility worked in alliance with the crown. He did wage one short and highly successful war, and conducted a successful diplomacy with his European neighbours, especially with England. He also presided over a period of almost unparalleled expansion in the Scottish economy. While some of these positive factors can be attributed to good fortune, especially the buoyant economy, others were unquestionably a matter of the king's personal abilities. But they do not make him a paragon of kingly virtues, on whom God showered his blessings. Indeed, contemporaries recorded the years of famine and failing harvests in his reign, and spoke of the deaths of his children as God's justice for the king's immoral and unprincipled ways. One chronicler described the king as a lecherous libertine, who whiled away his evening hours in drinking wine – he left unpaid a hefty bill for Bordeaux claret for which his successors were to be pursued – and in clandestine visits to nunneries where his objective was not religious devotion. While surely the medieval equiv-alent of tabloid 'news', these presumably scurrilous tales serve to remind us that, beneath the golden gloss, Alexander III was only human.

10

MARGARET

(1286-1290)

There is surely no more poignant passage in Scottish history than the tragically short 'reign' of this child monarch. Although traditionally styled 'queen' Margaret was never inaugurated and was more properly styled 'lady of Scotland'. Margaret's mother, also Margaret, only daughter of Alexander III and his first queen, Margaret of England, had married King Eric II Magnusson of Norway (1280-99), in Bergen cathedral in September 1281. This match had set the seal on Norway's developing good relations with her North Sea neighbours, Scotland and England, and sought to draw a line under the breakdown in Scoto-Norwegian relations that had occurred in the 1260s. The match soon proved fruitful and Princess Margaret was born in early April 1283, probably in Tönsberg on the coast south of Oslo. All too typically, Margaret's mother, aged around sixteen, died during or shortly after childbirth. This left her daughter's future firmly in the hands of the leading magnates of the day like Bishop Navre of Bergen rather than under the authority of her weak father, Eric, who only turned fifteen in 1283. Margaret was undoubtedly destined to play an important part through marriage in Norwegian foreign policy: the beginnings of her education in Bergen surely reflected this future role. But the untimely deaths of Alexander III's surviving son and heir in January 1284 and then of the Scottish king himself in March 1286 propelled Margaret into the first rank of desirable heiresses.

69. Both sides of the Great Seal appointed for the Government of the Realm after the death of Alexander III.

70. Birgham, Scottish Borders, where the Scots assembled in 1290 to ratify the marriage treaty of their future queen, Margaret, to the son of Edward I of England.

In parliament in March 1284 Alexander III had required his subjects to recognise the 'illustrious girl Margaret... as our lady and right heir of our said lord king of Scotland.' When the king perished this promise was honoured: for the first time, six Guardians (two earls, two bishops, two barons) were chosen to govern Scotland in the name of the 'community of the realm', not least because this was the lawful way to avoid full-blown civil war between the rival Scottish claimants to the throne, the houses of Balliol and Bruce, who resented – or sought to exploit – the succession of a mere foreign girl. For their part, the Norwegians were keen to secure Margaret's succession to recover control of the Western Isles and various unpaid monies. But it is clear that it was her great-uncle, Edward I of England, who really began to push the key matter of who would be Margaret's husband and thus King of Scots. In doing so Edward may have acted on Alexander III's hint of 1284 that his grand-daughter might wed the English king's son and heir, Edward (born April 1284), leading to a peaceful union of the English and Scottish crowns.

It was Edward as statesman who oversaw the treaty of Salisbury (November 1289) whereby Margaret was to be brought to the British Isles as yet un-betrothed and only when Scotland was 'at peace'. The various interested parties were competing doggedly for control of Margaret's person and kingdom, with the Bruces, Comyns and Balliol perhaps even hoping to wed their own heirs to the princess. Edward I and Eric II, however, were set on their match, with the English king even going so far in May 1289 as to secure papal approval for his son's marriage before the terms were finalized with the Scots. It was the treaty of Birgham of July 1290 between Edward, Eric and the Guardians which concluded that Prince Edward would wed Margaret and hold Scotland as a kingdom completely 'separate and divided' from England.

With the deal done, Edward I dispatched lavishly supplied ships to fetch the young bride to England. Yet in late August 1290 Margaret left Bergen – amidst much ceremony – in a Norwegian vessel bound for Orkney under the care of Bishop Navre. Here, on what would remain Norwegian soil until the 1460s, she was to be entrusted to an embassy of Scottish knights sent by William Fraser, bishop of St Andrews, as her escort to her inauguration at Scone: a silver bowl kept at Wemyss castle in Fife is said to be a relic of this mission. But by late September-early August the first rumours reached Scotland that Margaret had died of illness upon reaching the northern isle. She never saw Scotland and was returned for burial, after her distraught father had identified her body, in the cathedral church of Christ in Bergen (now destroyed).

In 1301 Eric II executed a false 'pretender' Margaret, giving rise to a minor martyr's cult. Later generations of Scots – beginning with the chronicler Andrew Wyntoun (*c.*1355-1422) – would lament the death of this innocent 'Maiden of Norway'. Scots and Norwegian ballads survive romanticizing the frail seven-year-old queen and her doomed journey: for example, the extremely popular (and possibly contemporary) northern folksong about 'Sir Patrick Spens', a seaman said to have been sent 'To Noroway, to Noroway' to bring princess Margaret to Scotland by King Alexander III himself. But in reality, in 1290 the Scots dwelt little on the little girl's fate as they became embroiled in conflict over the vacant throne.

SELECTED READING

GENERAL BACKGROUND

Barrow, G.W.S., *Kingship and Unity: Scotland 1000-1306* (London, 1981).

Duncan, A.A.M., *Scotland: the Making of the Kingdom* (Edinburgh, 1975).

Grant, A., *Independence and Nationhood: Scotland 1306-1469* (London, 1984).

Grant, A., and Stringer, K.J. (eds), *Medieval Scotland: Crown, Lordship and Community* (Edinburgh, 1993).

Mitchison, R., *From Lordship to Patronage: Scotland 1603-1746* (London, 1983).

Oram, R.D., *Scotland's Kings and Queens: Royalty and the Realm* (Edinburgh, 1997).

Smyth, A.P., *Warlords and Holy Men: Scotland AD 80-1000* (London, 1984).

Watson, F., *Scotland: A History 8000 BC – AD 2000* (Stroud, 2000).

Wormald, J., Court, *Kirk and Community: Scotland 1469-1625* (London, 1981).

THE HOUSE OF CANMORE

Barrow, G.W.S., *David I of Scotland (1124-1153): the Balance of New and Old* (Reading, 1984).

Oram, R.D. (ed.), *Scotland in the Reign of Alexander II* (Forthcoming, Glasgow, 2002).

Owen, D.D.R., *William the Lion. Kingship and Culture 1143-1214* (East Linton, 1997).

Reid, N. (ed.), *Scotland in the Reign of Alexander III* (Edinburgh, 1990).

Stringer, K.J., *The Reign of Stephen: Kingship, Warfare and Government in Twelfth-Century England* (London, 1993) [This gives a detailed account of David I's campaigns in northern England.]

Wilson, A.J., *St Margaret, Queen of Scotland* (Edinburgh, 1993).

LIST OF ILLUSTRATIONS

Cover Image: The initial letter M of Malcolm IV's great charter to Kelso
Abbey, with portraits of David I (left) and Malcolm himself.
Copyright Duke of Roxburghe.

16. St Rule's Tower. Copyright Richard Oram.
17. Alexander I's great seal image. Copyright Richard Oram.
18. Scone Abbey, great seal showing the inauguration of a Scottish king. Copyright Richard Oram.
19. David I from the initial letter M of Malcolm IV's great charter to Kelso Abbey. Copyright Richard Oram.
20. Drawing of one of the Lewis Chessmen found in 1831 on a beach in Lewis, in the Outer Hebrides. TA CD 8, 70.
21. David I as king and warrior. Copyright Richard Oram.
22. A silver penny of David I, minted from Cumbrian silver. Copyright Richard Oram.
23. Dryburgh Abbey, Borders. Copyright Richard Oram.
24. Kinloss Abbey, Moray. Copyright Richard Oram.
25. Kelso Abbey, Borders. Copyright Richard Oram.
26. The Tweed Valley from Wark Castle, Northumberland. Copyright Richard Oram.
27. Bamburgh Castle. Copyright Richard Oram.
28. Clitheroe Castle, Lancashire. Copyright Richard Oram.
29. Carlisle Castle, Cumbria. Copyright Richard Oram.
30. Malcolm IV from the intial letter M of his great charter to Kelso Abbey. Copyright Richard Oram.
31. William I as a mounted knight. Copyright Richard Oram.
32. Both sides of William I's seal. TA CD 14, 8 No 6 and TA CD 14, 9 No 7.
33. Prudhoe Castle, Northumberland. Copyright Richard Oram.
34. Falaise, Calvados. Copyright Richard Oram.
35. Henry II. TA CD 3, 37.
36. Berwick Castle, Northumberland. Copyright Richard Oram.
37. Arbroath Abbey, Angus. Copyright Richard Oram.
38. Seal of Arbroath Abbey, depicting the martyrdom of St Thomas of Canterbury. Copyright Richard Oram.
39. Drawing of the effigy of King John of England at Worcester Cathedral. TA CD Ormrod, Kings, p89.
40. Norham Castle, Northumberland. Copyright Richard Oram.
41. Balmerino Abbey, Fife. Copyright Richard Oram.
42. Tomb effigy, believed to be that of William I. Copyright Richard Oram.

INDEX

Flodden 1513
Niall Barr
'enthralling... reads as thrillingly as a novel.' *The Scots Magazine*
'an engrossing account of the battle... exemplary.'
BBC History Magazine
'the first modern analysis... a very readable account.'
Historic Scotland
'a very considerable achievement... fascinating and convincing.'
Military Illustrated
160pp 65 illus. Paperback
£14.99/$32.50   ISBN 0 7524 1792 4

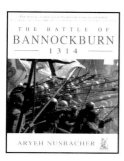

The Battle of Bannockburn 1314
Aryeh Nusbacher
'The most accessible and authoritative book on the battle.'
Dr Fiona Watson
'The first book on the Bannockburn campaign for almost a century...
recommended.'
Historic Scotland
176pp 73 illus. Paperback
£12.99/$18.99   ISBN 0 7524 2326 6

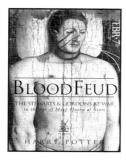

Bloodfeud
The Stewarts & Gordons at War in the Age of Mary Queen of Scots
Harry Potter
The story of a bloody feud between warring Scottish families in the
sixteenth century.
368pp 25 illus. Paperback
£17.99/$23.99   ISBN 0 7524 2330 4

Simply write, stating the quantity of books required and enclosing a cheque
for the correct amount, to: Sales Department, Tempus Publishing Ltd,
The Mill, Brimscombe Port, Stroud, Glos. GL5 2QG.

Alternatively, call the sales department on 01453 883300 to pay by Switch,
Visa or Mastercard.

US ORDERING

Please call Arcadia Publishing, a division of Tempus Publishing, toll free
on 1-888-313-2665

SCOTTISH HISTORY AVAILABLE FROM TEMPUS

The Kings & Queens of Scotland
Richard Oram (Editor)
'the colourful, complex and frequently bloody story of Scottish rulers…
an exciting if rarely edifying tale, told in a clear and elegant format.'
BBC History Magazine
'remarkable'
History Today
272pp 212 illus. (29 col) Paperback
£16.99/$22.99   ISBN 0 7524 1991 9

The Stewarts
Kings & Queens of Scotland 1371 - 1625
Richard Oram
The accessible illustrated history of the Stewart royal family, kings and
queens of the Scots from Robert II Stewart (1371-90) to James VI
Stewart (1567-1625), the last Stewart monarch to really know and
understand the Scots.
128pp 120 illus. Paperback
£10.99/$16.99   ISBN 0 7524 2324 X

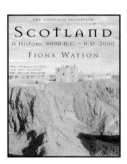

Scotland
A History 8000 B.C. - 2000 A.D.
Fiona Watson
A *Scotsman* Bestseller
'Lavishly illustrated throughout, its trenchant views, surprising revelations
and evocative descriptions will entrance all who care about Scotland.'
BBC History Magazine
A comprehensive history of a proud nation written by Scotland's answer
to Simon Schama, Fiona Watson, historian and presenter of BBC
Television's landmark history series *In Search of Scotland*.
304pp 100 illus. Paperback
£9.99/$14.99   ISBN 0 7524 2331 2

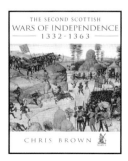

The Second Scottish War of Independence 1332-1363
Chris Brown
The least well known of Britain's medieval wars, the Second Scottish War
of Independence lasted for more than thirty years. The Scots were utterly
defeated in three major battles. So how did England lose the war?
208pp 100 illus. Paperback
£16.99/$19.99   ISBN 0 7524 2312 6